I0798994

HAUNTED NOBLE COUNTY INDIANA

MARK R. HUNTER AND EMILY JANE HUNTER

Haunted America

Published by Haunted America
A Division of The History Press
An imprint of Arcadia Publishing
Charleston, SC
www.historypress.com

First published 2025

Manufactured in the United States

ISBN 9781467156066

Library of Congress Control Number: 2025937581

Notice: The information in this book is true and complete to the best of our knowledge. It is offered without guarantee on the part of the authors or The History Press. The authors and The History Press disclaim all liability in connection with the use of this book.

CONTENTS

PREFACE

There are few people who haven't experienced something…strange. Unnatural. Supernatural, even. When The History Press approached us about writing another local history book, we didn't know that many ghost stories around Noble County. Still, we had a feeling that when we put the word out, plenty of others would.

We were right.

Ghost stories came out of the woodwork—also out of the basement, the attic, the cemetery and every hill worth calling a hill. It's not our business to decide which stories are true and which aren't, or even whether any *could* be true. We're just letting the people who shared them be heard.

In the end, this book is about all those who experienced or shared ghost stories, whether they chose to remain anonymous or not. It might also be wise to credit, if they exist, the ghosts themselves. After all, they started it—and they may just be our ancestors.

The area's first recorded white settlers, Joel Bristol and his family, arrived in what became Noble County in 1827, eleven years after Indiana became a state. As was common in the American frontier, a lot of tragedy and bad behavior followed, and by the time Noble County was officially organized eight years later, its sparse population was already accumulating stories to tell.

But of course, they weren't the first people in northeast Indiana. The Natives preceded them, and another civilization made the area home before that. Some of those earlier Natives were, shall we say, unusually tall—or so the stories go.

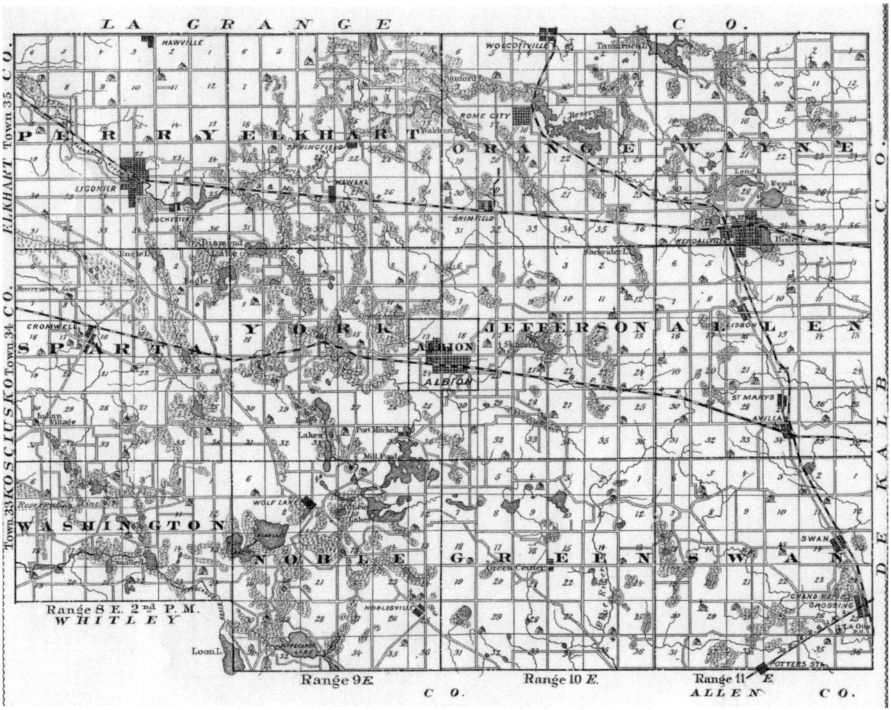

An 1876 map of Noble County, Indiana. *Noble County Historical Society.*

People are people, so there's not much doubt that all those populations had their own ghost stories. Sadly, they weren't written down. That's why most of our tales date to only the European settlement, when people arrived with lots of tales from the Old World to begin with.

Our book is divided generally by the locations where there are ghost stories—and where you think there would be. Often, those two don't connect, which can come as a surprise to those expecting the clichéd. The Noble County Courthouse, which stands tall in the very center of the county, was built where two other courthouses had already stood. The first burned with the help of persons unknown and came close to taking the rest of Albion with it. The second went out not with a blaze but with a whisper. The third has stood since 1888 and indeed has some stories to go with it—but no ghost stories.

So it goes with the old Noble County Jail, now the Old Jail Museum. Most of the area's cemeteries don't give anyone the heebie-jeebies, with the possible exception of daring teenagers late at night. One of the authors of

The 1889 New Hope Hospital, one of the many small hospitals that sprung up in early Noble County. It has since been divided to hold apartments and businesses. *Mark Hunter*.

this book, Mark, once lived in what used to be an early hospital without a single bump in the night.

What location does bring on tales of terror? Often, private homes. That's where many of their occupants passed on back in the day. Also, schools, businesses and even Kendallville's long-standing movie theater hold some haunted tales. Maybe ghosts stay close to the places where they spent most of their time or the best of their time.

You may wonder what proof there is that ghosts exist in one or any of these locations. Often, although not always, there is none. The statements of witnesses are all we have. That being the case, you might want to take these tales with a grain of salt. If you're a believer, you might want to take them with a ring of salt around you, just in case.

Either way, these tales are a lot of fun—just not always for the people who experienced them.

Acknowledgements

It would take a whole book to mention all the people who stepped forward to tell their tales or the tales of others—or to just point us in the right direction. We thank them and those who made photos available for us.

People who love ghost stories are often the same people who love history. It's all telling old stories, isn't it? Or sometimes, newer stories about old people. That being the case, many of those who helped with our previous history research also provided resources that helped out here. They include the Noble County Historical Society and Old Jail Museum, the Stone's Trace Historical Society, the Noble County Genealogical Society, the Noble County Public Library, the Kendallville and Ligonier Public Libraries and the Ligonier Historical Society.

We couldn't begin to list all the people who've contacted us with their own stories, stories passed down to them or just something they heard while sitting around a campfire. If, after taking all these notes, we miss someone's tale, we sincerely apologize. Also, although we made every effort to put the word out about this project, we're sorry if someone with a story or photos didn't get the word in time.

Thanks to John Rodrigue of The History Press, who guided us through the process and was very patient when disaster befell us, as it often did. Thanks also goes to:

Albion New Era newspaper
Arthur F. Mapes
Dean Leatherman
Jennifer Steffey
Kay Mapes Mason
Kendallville News-Sun newspaper

Kendallville Public Library
Kendallville Windmill Museum
Ligonier Public Library
Lori Wilson Gagen
Michael Ray Mapes
Noble County Genealogical Society
Noble County Historical Society
Noble County Public Library
Old Jail Museum of Noble County
Sarah Knopp, Noble County historian
Among many others!

1
Restless Natives and the Pre-History of Noble County

Paleo-Indians lived in Indiana before the people we usually think of as Natives. Research into these people is fascinating, but we'll spend only a moment here, because if those people chose to stick around as spirits, they've drifted away in more modern times.

Still, the Paleo-Indians left behind a few things that could be woven into a good supernatural tale. They were here as early as the Archaic period, around eight thousand years ago. Modern archeology seems to keep pushing that date back. This was the end of the last ice age, and the original occupants of the Midwest were almost certainly happy to see the glaciers retreat.

They might not have been so happy that the glaciers left a quarter of Indiana covered with swamps.

Over a period between then and around 1650 CE, the Natives built mounds and other earthworks of various sizes all across the region. Not surprisingly, Europeans who later settled the area referred to these people as the "Mound Builders." Sometimes, the earth moving was done for religious or defensive purposes, but more often, it seemed to be part of burial traditions.

Who knows? Maybe they were trying to keep their dead above the level of the swamps. If so, this didn't work well. While many bones have been discovered by zealous scientists, historians and locals, most are too decayed to be removed and preserved.

Then there were the giants.

Natives—the more recent Natives we usually think of—had stories of giants that lived in the Midwest before they arrived. One set of remains, found in Elkhart Township during a 1912 road construction project, was reputed to be nine feet tall. (Another newspaper story says it was found in 1899.) An investigator measured the thigh bone at eighteen inches long; this is close to average these days but would have made this person very tall hundreds of years ago.

The story goes that another giant was successfully recovered in 1893 and put on display at the office of Dr. Engles in Albion, where people were welcome to see it. We assume he didn't charge for an office visit. Reportedly, the skeleton was shipped to the Smithsonian Institute in Washington, D.C., to be examined further…where it vanished.

If you're into conspiracy theories, you may already know this wasn't the only such discovery that disappeared after arriving at the capital.

Were there giants? It depends on your point of view. Many witnesses said the giants of Indiana were seven to eight feet tall. Surely, this was some sort of supernatural race.

Not necessarily. It turns out, Natives of the time, especially those of the Great Plains, were some of the tallest people in the world. Many surprised white explorers discovered the Natives towered over them. It's possible the "mystery" of a few seven-foot-tall giants is no more unusual than a high school with a good basketball team.

The earthen structures made by the Mound Builders are fact, and many still stand. The Mound Builders' heights remain a matter of debate.

Considering the number of Mound Builder skeletons that were dug up by overzealous settlers, you would think their ghosts would be all over America. Alas, even those who followed close behind them had little to say about their predecessors.

Those who followed were, of course, the better-known Natives, often called Indians thanks to the confusion of Christopher Columbus. Many tribes had connections to Noble County, and many Native villages were occupied around the area. However, thanks to a treaty that made southwest Noble County part of a Native reservation, there's only one Indian Village today.

When the federal government forced the Natives onto that reservation, they agreed to build for Chief Wawaassa (also called Flat Belly) his own council house/residence, which became the first brick home constructed in Noble County. Ironically, after a tornado took that house down several years later, early white settlers used its bricks to build their own chimneys.

Now, one would think there *should* be at least one Native ghost haunting the Indian Village area. Flat Belly passed away and was replaced in 1837

Village Lake, the location of the earliest recorded drowning in Noble County, was near one of the county's last Native settlements. *Emily Hunter.*

by Mushquaw, who unfortunately had an affinity for whiskey. It was "poor" whiskey, the story goes.

The inebriated Mushquaw tried to cross a small lake nearby, which is now imaginatively called Village Lake. Halfway across, he had a "Hey, y'all, watch this!" moment, and while standing in the canoe, he tried to do a dance.

It didn't work out for him.

The reservation's medicine man later gave a speech in which he warned the dead chief not to get drunk while crossing the river of death to the spirit land. Maybe Mushquaw listened, and that's why people today don't hear his last song and dance floating across the water.

There followed an unrelated chain of tragedy, in which a young Native killed a female relative of the new chief, Kymotee, with a knife and then was immediately shot by Chief Kymotee. The original murderer's brother then shot Kymotee and was, in turn, killed by a witness.

How that didn't generate any ghosts is beyond belief, especially since the actual Native village's wigwams were later torched by white settlers and the site of the village is now Indian Village Cemetery.

Indian Village Cemetery was laid out where a Native village once stood. *Emily Hunter.*

The Native people in Indiana told their own story of mysterious beings who were not taller but substantially shorter than the average. These beings were called the Pukwudgies. Both the Natives and, later, the white settlers claimed to spot these beings, described as being only around three feet tall with blond hair that resembled a helmet. Maybe the Vikings got this far after all.

Witnesses said they were mischievous and curious but seemed to harbor no ill will aside from playing tricks on people.

Certainly, they weren't as scary as the much taller, hairy monster reported in other parts of Indiana, who left footprints twice the size of humans'—sure sounds a lot like a sasquatch.

But these creatures weren't ghosts, so they get only a mention—unless they became spirits upon death, giving a whole new angle to bigfoot stories.

2

Mysterious Disappearances

When the first white settlers arrived in what is now Noble County in 1827, they faced dark swamps and dense forests—not to mention the sometimes unfriendly Natives they were supplanting. It was like a Stephen King novel with mosquitoes, and Joel Bristol faced it with just his wife and her six orphaned nephews and nieces.

By some accounts, more than three years passed before another settler arrived.

But the Bristols lived on the superhighway of the time, a former Native trail then called the Fort Wayne and Goshen Road, located about halfway between the nearest settlements in Fort Wayne and Elkhart County. (Bristol settled near what is now Merriam.) It was widened for military use, possibly by troops under General "Mad" Anthony Wayne, which could explain why a cannon ball was found in the vicinity of Merriam. In 1913, it became part of the coast-to-coast Lincoln Highway. In 1919, a military convoy crossed through Noble County on an experimental trip across the country. It was a journey so difficult that it inspired one of its members, Dwight Eisenhower, to later create the interstate highway system.

When Noble County was founded, travel was of the slower animal variety, so trips that are now quick and easy were then long and arduous. That made Bristol's homestead the perfect—and only—place for settlers to stop for the night. Joel Bristol, his wife, and the Tibbott orphans did what anyone would have done: they started a tavern.

Built in 1876 as a residence, the Kimmell House Inn is an example of the businesses that sprang up along the Lincoln Highway to serve weary travelers. *Mark Hunter*.

Maybe *roadhouse* would be a better term. Built on one of Noble County's rolling hills, the location became known as Rowdy Ridge due to the drinking and carousing that went on there. It should come as no surprise that a man who was willing to move his family into the wilderness would be a gambler.

So, this was the setting when, in 1828, a mounted traveler arrived for the night. According to lore, the traveler was unusually well dressed and had full saddle bags, as well as the happy expression of a prosperous man. He rode up to the Bristol Tavern to find both Natives and white men heavily into liquor-fueled revelry, complete with singing and card games.

The man, the story goes, intended to be on his way the next morning. Instead, he got drawn into the celebrating, and by the fourth evening, he had gambled away everything—his money, horse and even his coat and hat. At twilight, someone noticed him staggering into the darkening forest. Maybe they thought he was just headed to relieve himself or possibly bang his head against a tree.

He was never seen again.

The entire story wasn't told until many years later, probably out of fear that someone who played cards with the unknown man might be blamed for his death. In a way, they were to blame. Still, this man was hardly the last person who vanished into the woods and swamps of Noble County.

According to local legend, a creek south of Albion got its name from another disappearance. The swamps surrounding it were as dangerous as a swamp can get, and one day, a man and his horse proved this. The story is handed down that a man named Lewis, while riding down the banks of that branch, suddenly disappeared into quicksand in the dead of night—horse and all—and was never seen again.

From then on, the waterway was called Lewis' Branch, although we assume he'd rather have gained fame in a different way. To add insult to injury, even that was taken away from the lost soul; the general path of the former Lewis' Branch is now the straighter and more controlled Croft Ditch.

Other sources say the branch was named after Lewis Potts in 1836, the year he arrived in Noble County, but we like the spookier version better. Or could they be the same person? But no, the more well-known Lewis lived until 1850 and died of "consumption," not quicksand.

Three years after Joel Bristol claimed a homestead, around 1830, more settlers arrived in the west-central part of the county. One of those settlers, John L. Powers, had the idea of starting his own roadhouse in Perry Township. But it was his Sparta Township neighbor Richard Stone's name that became synonymous with a tavern. Powers, who, for a time, lived in a Sparta Township cave before establishing his business, gave up and moved west after a few years. Stone stayed in business for so long that his tavern still stands today, although not in the same place.

Early settlers in Noble County provided the infrastructure to support the settlers who traveled *through* Noble County. The floodgates for settlement opened after that, and as more and more settlers stayed to put down roots in Noble County, they, of course brought their families with them.

That led to tragedy in 1841, not far from the future Lincoln Highway.

Early on June 2, Aaron Noe left his Cromwell area homestead, headed for a mill in Elkhart County. Not long after he set out, he caught sight of his three-year-old son following the wagon, so he shooed the boy toward home and went on his way.

Three-year-olds are not so easily shooed.

When the family's other children returned home, the boy was not with them. Mrs. Noe and the children found the child's footprints on the road, but soon they disappeared. Word went out to the closest neighbors, and from there, it traveled to neighbors farther away, and by nightfall, close to

Stone's Tavern, one of the first businesses in Noble County, has been the center of the Stones Trace Pioneer Festival since 1973. *Stones Trace Historical Society.*

Larger wild animals almost became extinct in Indiana, but now, deer, foxes and coyotes roam Noble County, producing hair-raising sounds at night. *Emily Hunter.*

one hundred settlers had joined the search. That was probably about all the settlers in the area at the time.

The road ran near Solomon's Creek, which was surrounded by a swampy forest that was home to timber wolves, wild hogs and clouds of insects that were themselves dangerous at the time. There were also still plenty of Natives, and no love was lost between them and the settlers. A small group of Natives had passed earlier, and some settlers tracked them to their camp on Bowen Lake, now a part of Chain o' Lakes State Park. But the surprised Natives didn't have the child.

For over a week, every inch of ground around the farmstead was searched, but tragically, no sign of the child was ever found.

There were several animals in Indiana at the time that sometimes sounded like crying babies, and some of those animals are still around today. If you hear one late one night, that's probably all it is—not the ghost of a lonely child trying to find home.

Probably.

3
House of Spirits

Where are ghosts most likely to be found? One of the authors of this book (Mark) once lived in a former hospital and slept in what had been a patient room. His medical doctor's current office is located in a former funeral home, and he and Emily love taking walks through cemeteries. That last hobby might seem a bit morbid, but it's peaceful—at least during the day.

And yet, the only possible spooky experiences either author had occurred in homes.

Emily's experience occurred in Missouri with some stereotypically friendly ghosts who just wanted people to know they were there. She also has a tale of a house with bones in the wall—human bones. Mark was at a home in Kendallville when someone started bouncing a ball upstairs, but he was the only person awake in the house.

We must remember that, until relatively recently, most people died not in medical care facilities but in their own homes. Places where people live have always been places where people die, too—something to think about if you live in an old house.

One of the earliest recorded house hauntings in Noble County involved Mitchell McClintock, one of the men who accosted traveling Natives while searching for the lost toddler in 1841. McClintock and a man named Obadiah Tilton were early settlers to the area, but they didn't settle legally. A part of Noble County was still a Native reservation, and the two men built their homes inside Native territory, in what is now Sparta Township.

An 1840s-era log cabin was moved from its original home in Dekalb County to Stones Trace, now a National Historic Site. *Mark Hunter*.

The time came, of course, when the Natives were kicked out. In 1842, their former lands were opened to settlement by, let's face it, invaders from the east. That should have allowed the two squatters and their families to breathe easy, but there was still the matter of making it legal. McClintock and Tilton didn't jump fast enough. According to the 1882 book *Counties of Lagrange and Noble*, as soon as the lands became available, a man named George Platter rushed to the land office to enter both of the farms as his own property.

It was a dirty deed, you might say. But it was also a legal one, which caused the McClintock and Tilton families to be evicted from their own homesteads. Efforts by the Indiana state legislature to allow squatters to keep their land didn't help in this case.

McClintock died not long after, and his friends blamed his death on being cheated out of his land. He and his widow received nothing for the work they had done in starting their farms. (Yes, the farms were illegal, but even back then, two wrongs didn't make a right.)

That's why, whenever someone happened to pass by the old McClintock home around midnight, they would hear a melancholy voice commanding, "Pay the widow—pay the widow!"

Sadly, no one ever did.

REPORTING ON A REPORTER

In more modern times, an Albion family experienced a not-at-all frightening ghost who may have just been continuing the work she did in life. Mary Robinson Smith lived with her family on East Hazel Street, and she said, "We presume she [the spirit] was the past owner who had died in the house—we had less than ten sightings, which were all unthreatening."

Who could this peaceful spirit be? The only thing anyone saw was a whitish chiffon image, nothing specific. Mary thinks she knows the spirit's identity after an experience with two children she babysat for at the home. After being dropped off, they'd go back to sleep for a few hours. "When they got up, they asked me what I was doing after they settled in....They heard typing."

But Mary hadn't been typing.

Her conclusion: the spirit was Alice Gagen, a former resident of the home who, in life, typed quite a lot. And what was Alice doing? Getting the newspaper ready, of course.

Alice Gagen, a Central Noble schoolteacher who passed away in 1981, was the assistant publisher of the Albion weekly newspaper, *Noble County American*, along with her husband, Robert. The Gagen family is well known to the authors of this book. In addition to publishing the paper, Bob served as the president of the Noble County Historical Association. The Gagens' daughter Sarah was the secretary at that same organization and followed her father as Noble County historian, and her husband, Dave Knopp, was a reporter for the *Kendallville News-Sun* before he passed away.

In other words, the Gagen family was heavily involved in their community and never turned their backs on hard work. It makes sense that Alice Gagen would still be working on the next edition in spirit.

HOMELY SPIRITS

Ormas is a small collection of buildings, mostly homes, that straddles the Whitley County line in southwest Noble County. That's where Amanda Mulkey and her family lived, and when Amanda was a child, her mother would get up at about 3:00 a.m. for work. Several times, Amanda's mother saw a figure that would check on Amanda as she slept. It was a nonthreatening figure, thank goodness. Apparently, the only bad thing that spirit did was play hide and seek. "We had items that would come up missing, only to show up months later in really bizarre spots, like a couch that we never moved."

Child ghosts are common figures in many stories, and one from the Albion area seems especially creepy. A resident of a farmhouse along River Road said a child ghost inhabited their basement, and they occasionally found her crying in a corner. The witness goes on to say the little girl, dressed in old-time clothes, eventually showed up in their parents' upstairs closet, sitting on the floor, grinning at the living people.

For some reason, the idea of the child smiling makes the story even more creepy.

Relatively benign spirits seem to be active in many older residences across Noble County. Cindy Weber reported having a few ghostly encounters when she lived in an Albion home at the intersection of First and South Streets. But that ghost may not have originated with a single-family residence; according to local lore, the building was part of a hotel, since moved from its spot uptown.

That's exactly what happened to the Worden House, a former hotel that was divided into three structures and moved to various locations across town.

The Worden House Hotel was moved from Port Mitchel to Albion and later partitioned into three homes—one of which is possibly haunted. *Noble County Historical Society.*

(This was the second move for the building, which was first transported from Port Mitchell when the county seat was moved from there to Albion.)

The Worden House barely survived the fire that burned Albion's courthouse in 1859. While protecting their hotel, one of the Worden brothers slipped and fell from the roof, fracturing both of his legs. For all we know, the Worden brothers might still occupy a former section of their business to continue protecting it.

Cindy Weber reports that her home's TV would sometimes switch itself on, a common thing in ghost stories—after all, the ghosts can't turn the pages of a book, so they need some entertainment. At one point, in the same building, a witness saw a man wearing an old-style suit and derby hat.

It's always possible Albion, the Noble County seat, has more than the average number of haunted houses. A former Albion volunteer firefighter told the story of seeing a man dressed in antique firefighting clothing standing in his living room, bending over to examine the living occupant's fire alert pager. The house was certainly old enough to have been occupied at a time when almost every able-bodied male was a member of the department. Maybe this man was thinking about how useful it would have been to have a pager instead of the bell at the firehouse.

On a firefighting-related note, we've been assured by more than one firefighter that *all* the Kendallville fire stations are haunted—not only the

Built in 1907, the Kendallville Fire Department and City Hall burned seven years later. The ghosts, if they were already there, stuck around in the new firehall. *Mike Mapes collection.*

original Station One downtown, but also the second station along U.S. 6 and the newer Station One, which was built not far from a reported haunted house where the East Noble Middle School now stands. Can ghosts migrate? It depends on who you ask.

Firefighters say they've heard footsteps, doors opening and closing and voices, all where there was no one to make them. "That place was just creepy," one firefighter said of the 1914 firehouse, now a part of the Kendallville Police Department (which makes the spirits the problem of the police now). It should be noted that the 1914 building wasn't really the first firehouse; it replaced the original 1907 city hall/firehouse, which, perhaps ironically, burned in early 1914. The replacement became the first Station One when the second firehouse was built decades later.

One theory is that the firetrucks brought back with them the spirits of the people who died at emergency scenes. That's a number that would, unfortunately, add up over the years. We're not aware of any reports of spirits in Noble County's other dozen or so current and former firehouses, but we wouldn't be surprised if there were other ghosts there.

4
GRAND OLD HOUSE

Like many people of her time, Jesta Parks never strayed far from her home. And why should she? By all accounts, the three-story home south of the Mt. Pleasant Church in Jefferson Township was a grand place to live.

But Jesta didn't just live there. She also died there, and she didn't bother to leave then either.

Bridget Ammond Frey not only alerted us to this tragic story, but she also once lived in the home. She also met Jesta…after Jesta died.

We met with Bridget Frey beside Jesta Parks's grave in the Mt. Pleasant Cemetery, a stone's throw from the location of her home. In keeping with the story, Jesta's body never strayed far from the house either, perhaps a third of a mile or so, with both her grave and the house on the west side of the road. Jesta, born in 1879, was laid to rest there in 1939, after she hanged herself in her own home. Maybe "rest" isn't the best way to phrase it.

Bridget and her husband, Rick, moved into the residence in 1986, not realizing it was already occupied. Bridget described the home, which was built in 1885, as ornate and sturdy, with oak timbers brought up from Fort Wayne and a grand open staircase. It was still heated with a wood-burning stove, and Bridget had to get the fire going every morning. Clearly, *opulent* meant something different back then, but it still applied.

Jesta Parks, of course, arrived long before Bridget did. Jesta's father, Lambert McFarland, was one of Noble County's earliest pioneers, a well-respected farmer with about 250 acres of land where he built the house. In

1872, he married Frances E. Barhan, which brings us back to their daughter, Jesta, along with their son, Owen.

It should be noted that when Jesta's father, Lambert, passed in 1910, he died in the same home—although that's not germane to this story, is it?

When Jesta married Merton J. Parks, they stayed in her father's home, which was not unusual. They also apparently had no children, which *was* unusual. Whether she suffered from depression over not having children or another mental health issue was never reported. All we know is that on May 9, 1939, M.J. Parks arrived home at lunchtime to discover Jesta had tied a rope around her neck and flung herself from the third-story attic area into the stairwell. She was sixty-one.

We can only speculate about why she chose to end her own life. However, we might take a hint from one detail Bridget told us: when her family moved in, they found a casket upstairs—an unused casket.

It was a children's casket.

Having a casket of any size just lying around wasn't much more normal then than it is today. Again, we can only speculate about how it came to be there, but if it was there when Jesta died, it surely speaks to her mental state.

As we said, Bridget knew nothing of this when she moved in. But not long after, she found in the house an *Albion New Era* newspaper article. It contained an obituary detailing how Jesta had died, which must have come as quite a shock, to say the least. Still, the death had occurred almost fifty years before Bridget moved in—surely there was nothing to be upset about after all this time.

And there wasn't…at first.

After doing some quick math, Bridget says it was 1989, when her son Caleb was about fourteen months old, when odd things began happening. She had gone up on the attic stairs to hide Christmas presents. With her son so young, she hadn't had to conceal presents before, and she rarely went into the attic for anything. Since no one else went up there either, it was an excellent hiding place.

That's what she was doing when Caleb let out a blood-curdling scream. Running downstairs, Bridget noticed the television was on. This was not a big deal, except Bridge never watched TV.

Also, the TV screen was glowing green.

For those of you who weren't around when televisions got their signal from antennas, this was not normal. She described it as a glowing almost neon green, the same kind of color some people have experienced during tornado weather.

In the Mount Pleasant Cemetery, not far from where she died, Jesta Parks was laid to rest. Or was she? *Emily Hunter.*

The baby was fine, but it didn't take Bridget long to figure out she was dealing with the supernatural. Remember, Jesta never had any children of her own. Could it be that her spirit had leaned in for a look, maybe too close for the baby's comfort? Some say infants can see things adults can't. That's not something that seems logical, of course, but the spirit world laughs in the face of logical.

We would assume Bridget doesn't have a lot of experience watching ghost stories on TV, considering she doesn't watch TV. What she does have is the plain-speaking, no-nonsense attitude that older generations assume once they've seen enough to have seen everything.

So, Bridget simply sat down and had a talk with the ghost.

She offered Jesta a deal: "You leave my kids alone; I'll leave your attic alone."

And that was the last time spirits ever bothered her children.

But Jesta didn't leave. As often happens with people after their first experience with the supernatural, Bridget could feel Jesta's presence in the house. Jesta was always around.

In 2012, Bridget's husband, Rick, died, and the family had a bonfire outside as a way to say goodbye. There, outside at the bonfire, a guest heard a woman talking about children—heard, but didn't see.

Jesta was clearly unhappy, and since, by then, the internet had become a thing, Bridget looked for a solution online. At the time, she still included her phone number along with her name on her automatic email signature, which prompted a call from a spirit removal expert in the Carolinas. He could do the job, he said, for less than $200.

Bridget's reply was that she could do it herself for much less—so she did.

At the time, no one was living in the house, so Bridget showed up with some candles and an appeal to the spirits. It was pretty basic stuff; she asked Jesta to move on. Bridget also, not surprisingly, under the circumstances, asked her deceased husband, Rick, to send her a sign that everything was OK.

When Bridget went back to her car, she found a heart-shaped aspen leaf glowing on the ground by her car door.

Except the sun wasn't shining. And there were no aspen trees nearby.

Bridget still has that leaf, pressed and sealed. Clearly, Rick sent her the sign she desired.

But did Jesta Parks really leave?

Bridget was riding with a neighbor one day, and as they passed the still-unoccupied house, she saw that it was occupied by a woman sitting by an upstairs window. Bridget mentioned this to a neighbor and could tell by his reaction that he knew what she was talking about. He'd seen the spirit before, too. That makes the rest of the home's story that much more interesting.

The house was sold to a man we won't name (for reasons that will become apparent). To this day, Bridget is upset about what happened next. The new owner stripped the house to its bones, taking the expensive woodworking and everything else until there was nothing left but a bare skeleton. What was left lingered for a while, but eventually, the frame of the home was torn down, leaving behind a little wooded area with a small pond on one corner of the property.

Not long after removing everything that made the house a home, the man responsible was found dead on his couch, Bridget says. He was fifty-five years old. Coincidence? Or was Jesta Parks protecting her home one last time?

5

Neighborhood Spirits

Tyson Fry once lived in a small mobile home park along West Hazel Street in Albion, in a home he said was brand-new at the time. That's one reason why he thinks the supernatural activity is connected to the land there rather than the building.

About a week after he moved in, "things started to happen," and they continued to happen until the day he moved out. He didn't say anything to other family members when, while in bed late one night, he heard a silverware drawer being pulled out and someone digging around as they were looking for a spoon—or knife.

Then he heard footsteps coming down the hallway.

Tyson got up and waited against the wall to jump the intruder when they got to the bedroom door. As soon as the footsteps arrived, he jumped out, fists at the ready, just to see—nothing.

When he turned on the light, he learned his wife was awake. She'd heard the same noises.

For a time, Tyson worked at night and slept during the day, which you'd think would be good in a haunted place. But while sleeping on the couch, he'd start hearing someone rummaging through unpacked boxes in the spare bedroom. This is annoying when you're trying to sleep—even more so when you're alone in the house.

The activity continued, with cupboard doors being opened and strange noises occurring in the night. Tyson said that when his father stopped by, the older man made fun of the situation by telling the ghost to turn off the TV. "Not even ten seconds go by, and the TV shuts off. The remote was on the table in front of me."

A more frightening moment came when the family's young daughter, around five or six years old, rushed up to her parents and said, "The man told me to get out of my room."

Insomnia led to another encounter. When Tyson woke up around midnight, he decided to have a smoke and went out to his car, where the cigarettes were in the center console. But as he rummaged around in the car, the open car door suddenly closed. He looked up, and in the rearview mirror, he saw a police officer standing there with a flashlight.

Thinking the officer might be about to bust him for a car burglary, Tyson opened the car door and turned to explain the situation to the officer. But the man wasn't there. "I'll never forget that face," Tyson said of the phantom officer.

Perhaps it was a ghost cop patrolling a haunted neighborhood.

Tyson, who wisely no longer lives there, was later told that a little girl haunts a house near the mobile home park. What's more frightening, the idea that a whole area is haunted or a little girl ghost?

We still maintain that a child spirit is the scarier of the two.

Haunted Avilla

Like in Albion, there's a location in Avilla, other than a home, that might have spirit activity. An anonymous poster on GhostsOfAmerica.com said they lived near Fourth Street and had a terrifying experience along a creek that runs through the town. They said they started to get a strange feeling when they let their dogs out at night; they felt like they weren't welcome but ignored it.

Finally, one night, the poster, who said their hair stood on end, listened to the feeling and headed for home. But as soon as they started to leave, their dog turned and began barking as if they were being threatened. There was nothing there—nothing visible.

The poster—and we approve wholeheartedly—ran, and from then on, they only approached the area during daylight. They think the creek itself was involved somehow. Who knows?

Another commentator said that when they requested it, a spirit spun a merry-go-'round at the Avilla Park about half a dozen times. This would be, we believe, the Eley Memorial Park on the other side of town. Considering the number of child ghosts that get reported, it's not hard to believe one of them might still be playing.

At least one person said they've had strange experiences at Oak Farm Middle School, which also stands not far from a stream, although the geography makes it hard to say if it's the same waterway.

It's not at all unusual to find reports of hauntings in or around bodies of water, with Noble County's Diamond Lake being one of them. A lot of tragedies happen in places where people underestimate the danger of water. This can lead to legends fed by the sometimes chilling sounds of animals and insects, the splash of unseen fish or winds blowing across the shoreline.

But who is doing the haunting? We can't be sure, but the Avilla Cemetery is located just a block from Eley Memorial Park, and the cemetery even has a creek bed running through it. Our candidate is John O. Scheurick, who, in 1896, was found dead in that cemetery. He was not just dead—he was newly dead.

The seventy-eight-year-old man was located draped across the tomb of his wife, and a coroner's inquest revealed that the wealthy man, who had no relatives nearby, had been despondent for weeks. An empty morphine bottle was found with him.

LAKE UN-LIFE

Let's leave Noble County for just a moment for the R-rated version of a haunted lake tale. One can easily find the story of Alice Marble Gray, who lived along Lake Michigan in a small shack. Alice was a naturalist in more ways than one. A free spirit, Alice was sometimes seen running naked along the shore or swimming in the cold water. In 1925, she was said to have been murdered, allegedly by the father of her two daughters, who had already been accused of another fatal attack.

Whether she was murdered at all, let alone by her husband, is not really certain. What is certain is that she led an interesting life, and it's a shame to have it boiled down to a naked ghost story. Still, that's where her fame lies, and various versions of her tragedy can easily be found.

To this day, Alice—often called "Diana of the Dunes," maybe just for the alliteration—can be seen still wandering the area she loved, in what is today the Indiana Dunes National Park, completely naked.

As far as we know, running around naked in a National Park is against the rules, but rules are one thing Alice never cared about.

6
Home Is Where the Haunt Is

Back to Noble County—and to homes. A few commenters, most of them anonymous, have talked about a haunted house on the east side of Avilla. This one was not occupied by a friendly ghost—not at all.

We're not sure of its exact location, but if it's where we think it is, the ditch mentioned in the earlier story might run nearby. And it is a spooky looking place, at least at night. An anonymous poster said that while they lived there, another resident was choked in their sleep. In addition, toys with no batteries suddenly started playing.

Even more frightening, a witness said they awoke one night and saw a legless man dressed in what appeared to be attire from the 1800s. The man was sitting, we assume. Another time, they came down the steps to find a woman, similarly dressed, staring up at them. The air always seemed thick and heavy, and their dog stayed at the top of the basement stairs, growling and barking into the darkness.

It's no wonder they didn't live there long.

Still another website poster spoke of what we believe is the same house—if it's not, there are two such homes close together, both described as being on a hill. This witness, who lived in the home for about four and a half years, said the previous two residents had reported the same activity: dark figures, voices at night, items coming up missing—and a feeling of evil in one of the bedrooms.

There's also reportedly the grave of an unknown Civil War soldier on the property, which would certainly explain a lot. Maybe he is the man who

Civil War reenactors escort a civilian at the Stones Trace Pioneer Festival. Noble County saw no Civil War battles, but many veterans were buried there. *Mark Hunter.*

lost his legs in battle? However, although we easily found a house that meets the description, we have yet to find the location of a solitary grave in that neighborhood.

A note in passing: a small town in Missouri named after Indiana's Avilla, is alleged to be completely haunted. The whole town. Located along Route 66, it was the scene of bloody conflicts during the Civil War, and it had its very own Hanging Tree.

Other Homes

Haunted houses abound, of course. One Noble County resident told us of a house along CR 300 East in Rome City, where she said a drum set in a back room once played on its own. That's unusual activity, as the ghost would have had to physically pick up the drumsticks. Meanwhile, occupants heard women screaming and doors shaking violently, saw a dark figure and even found birds flying into a toilet! To us, the last straw would have been when the owner heard someone running toward him—even though no one was there. The toilet thing is extra weird, though.

One day, at a home close to the Elkhart River, near Cosperville, a witness's grandmother got on the phone to her family, complaining that a vehicle had stopped in her driveway with its high beams shining at her. Relatives living next door walked right up to the woman's window, but she couldn't see her kin because of the lights—only there were no lights there.

The same witness reported seeing bright orbs floating through their woods along the river, sometimes faster than a person could run, along with other strange lights. Orbs are a common appearance in haunted places and can usually be explained—but not always.

A former Rome City resident posted anonymously that many years ago, they lived in a Rome City house so old that it didn't have indoor plumbing. To stay warm, they slept downstairs with the door to the area closed. Imagine their surprise when someone knocked on that door—from upstairs.

The first few times, they said, the knocks didn't scare them because they thought it was a real person who'd come in through an upstairs window. In our opinion, that would be just as scary—if not more so.

Finally, the knocks roused them, and they got up to see a woman with long, dark hair sitting in a chair at the bottom of the stairwell. Moments later, she disappeared without the witness getting a look at her face, which was maybe for the best.

Eventually, our anonymous hero had children of their own, and one night, they woke to see a man in a red and black plaid shirt standing over the kids' bed, just looking at them. Then he, too, disappeared. Years later, the home was torn down, but by then, the witness had, unsurprisingly, moved away.

We've always wondered what happens to homebound spirits when they lose their home. Are landfills full of dispossessed ghosts? What a depressing way to spend eternity.

A more peaceful occupation occurred in a LaOtto home. We haven't been able to confirm the location of the southeast Noble County residence, and the website where we first heard the tale no longer lists it. Perhaps the elderly man and his wife, who passed peacefully in the home, were just too boring to merit attention. Still, the home's occupants reportedly heard the voices of the two, and it's said one remains there, searching for his son.

Another example of peaceful coexistence comes from Kendallville, where an anonymous poster said they once lived in an upstairs apartment. Not knowing where this apartment is located, we do wonder if the building was once used for something else.

The witness started getting the feeling someone—or something—was sitting beside them, and often felt as if someone stood behind them, looking over their shoulder. Remember, most ghosts can't turn pages, so maybe they were just reading. Being braver than, say, us, the witness simply started talking to their guest spirit. At that point, they weren't scared, just confused, and eventually, the activity stopped.

That is, until a month later, when a friend came to spend the night. In the morning, they said they saw a little girl, seven to eight years old, with long, curly hair. They even described the child's dress: long sleeves, with lace around the collar and sleeves. The child stood there for several minutes and then disappeared.

We don't know if the friend ever returned, but the resident said they felt at peace after that.

Less peaceful was the experience of a new Noble County resident, who moved from Montana to an apartment in Rome City. As they were shown around the apartment complex, they noticed a few neighbors giving them strange looks, but they thought nothing of it. The looks may have had something to do with what their guide then told them: they would be moving into a residence where a murder had taken place a few years before.

This was not an old story or a vague rumor; the murder really did happen. A woman died, and her husband was eventually convicted of the crime.

But the new resident said that kind of thing didn't bother them, and the family loved the apartment and their new town.

Sure, things kept getting misplaced, but that happens, doesn't it? The TV remote would disappear most often. If that was being done by a ghost, then at least the spirit would helpfully turn the TV on and change the volume randomly, even when no one else was around.

Eventually, the living occupants started hearing people talking—and even loudly arguing—when no one was around. The last straw came when the renter started seeing a woman looking down at her from the top of the stairs. Other things may have occurred that they didn't want to talk about, but in any case, the family left the apartment one night and never came back. It's said they now live in Alaska, which is about the farthest they could get from Rome City without leaving the continental United States.

The only other thing we know about the apartment is that, according to neighbors, nobody lives there for long.

7
Spook Hill and the Children's Section

Spook Hill. You can't find a better name than that if you're looking for the supernatural.

There are at least three Spook Hills, a more famous one being located in Lake Wales, Florida. Thanks to an optical illusion there, cars that are turned off and shifted into neutral seem to roll uphill. A similar story comes from Spook Hill in New York State.

Our Spook Hill is officially named Sand Hill, the second highest named point in Indiana. (It doesn't look imposing, because the area it rises from is already at a high elevation.) It's north of Kendallville, near the LaGrange County line, and on its southeast slope is the isolated Weston Chapel Cemetery. The land was donated by a man named, yes, Weston. Whether he was directly involved in the legendary events on the hill is unknown.

Noble County youths would drive up the tree-lined lane and then climb the hill to the cemetery to tell some stories and get a good scare. It apparently became a challenge for area high schoolers, and the story goes that no one who tried to stay overnight lasted longer than one or two hours.

Many stories arose about Spook Hill over the years. Its infamy would certainly explain why the current owners have blocked the drive with a padlocked gate, especially after vandals broke many of the stones.

But there's a more specific tale about how Spook Hill became haunted, and it's not as innocent as a teenage ghost story: the legend of the Spook Hill Light. (There might be some confusion here involving a Spook Light Hill, farther south near Terra Haute. We have a Spook Hill Light; they have a Spook Light Hill.)

The story can be found in the Indiana University Archives, as related years ago by the *Kendallville News-Sun* newspaper, which got the story from a local gentleman, Alan Fordeck, who heard the tale thirty years earlier from an elderly resident named Elbert Lebeirnz. To stop the phone tag game, the Fordecks wrote the legend down in 1997. Avilla's Ruth Albaugh, who actually lived on Spook Hill as a little girl, guessed the original story was over 110 years old.

At the time, a farm stood near the crest of Sand Hill. A traveling salesman—technically a pack peddler, who carried his items in a backpack—came along late at night, looking for a place to stay. He had the misfortune of knocking on the farmhouse door.

Although the name of the farm's owner isn't reported, the unknown man was kind enough to allow the peddler to stay the night. Then, late at night, after the peddler fell asleep, the farmer revealed his unkind side.

He killed his guest and buried him in the home's cellar.

Why? The only clue we have is that the farmer was said to have been a heavy drinker and often arrived home drunk late at night. Or maybe he took up drinking after he committed the murder?

Either way, when he arrived home in times after the killing, he would pace up and down at the end of the driveway instead of going in. Something—or someone—prevented him from crossing it to get home. Sometimes, he was stuck outside all night, and Ruth Albaugh said his footprints would be visible the next morning. It was not until his wife would send their boy out to take his father by the hand that the farmer would be able to go inside.

Mrs. Albaugh's theory was that the spirit of the peddler (Is he still buried in the basement?) prevented his killer from getting sleep. Her own relatives refused to stay at the house, and the legend quickly spread.

Who was the murderous farmer anyway?

Without knowing exactly when the killing took place or where on the hill the house and barn stood, it's hard to tell. We know that in 1860, the entire hill was owned by Thomas B. Weston, who arrived in Noble County in 1842. By all accounts, Weston was a pillar of the community and unlikely to be our suspect.

At some point after that, the hill's ownership was split in two, north to south. In 1874, John Shifaly owned the west side, G. Friend owned the south part of the east side and J. Goodworth owned the north part of the east side. The cemetery was just west of the center of the hill, on Shifaly's property, although it now belongs to a cemetery trust.

If you'll forgive a quick historical aside: our research uncovered that John Shifaly arrived in Noble County from Germany, and in 1854, he was taken in by a descendent of one of the *Mayflower* colonists, Thomas B.—wait for it—Weston. One job benefit: eventually, Shifaly married Weston's daughter.

It was Weston who donated land for the cemetery and Shifaly who donated the land for the Weston Chapel. Maybe he felt guilty?

Shifaly later took over the operation of Weston's farm, expanded it and lived there for sixty or more years. Shifaly was a well-known teetotaler who avoided any form of alcohol, so he's also not a good candidate for our murderous farmer.

In 1893, another plat book shows Shifaly still lived there, but the entire east side was now owned by Henry Hutchins. But wait, a different source from 1893 shows A. Kreese lived on the west side, and R. Brennan lived on the east side. That's probably the same Adolf Kresse, the correct spelling (not Kreese), who owned the west side in the early 1900s, when the east side was divided between C.M. Turner and John Hutchins. Kresse remained the owner of the side that included the cemetery in 1941.

This is not to confuse the reader—although it definitely succeeds at that—but to show how hard it is to pin down a possible suspect in a possible murder that led to a haunted hill. We found matches for many of the names listed but nothing about any of them that hinted at criminal tendencies.

Worse, while we know where the chapel was located and where the cemetery is, it's difficult to say where the farm stood.

Eventually, the house collapsed from age, and the barn was leveled by arson. It was Al Fordeck who bought the property, where he planted a walnut grove. Fordeck laughed when Elbert Lebeirnz told him the story, but that didn't keep it from spreading.

Witnesses claimed that, since the time of the murder, a mysterious shape has been seen carrying a lantern from the barn to the house. Whether that continues now that both buildings are gone isn't certain, but visitors to Spook Hill still tell stories about mysterious happenings. Some claim when they parked on the lane that leads to the cemetery, their cars would randomly not start and then start again later.

Maybe the peddler is still looking for a ride off Spook Hill.

POET LAUREATE

There's another version of the legend of Spook Hill, and it seems to have been mixed up with a different ghost legend. Arthur F. Mapes, a former Indiana poet laureate and Kendallville resident, wrote a poem about the legend. The poem mentions an accused murderer being lynched, and this did indeed happen in Noble County—but at Diamond Lake Hill, not Spook Hill.

The poem is reprinted here with the permission of Arthur Mapes's daughter Kay Mapes Mason:

There's a story that old timers told
That always brings a thrill,
It was told to me by Sassafras John,
It's the Legend of Spook Hill.
This hill is jist a little west
Of the ol' brick Stony Ridge school.
Folks said, "The man who tarried there
Would find he was more than a fool."
But let's go back to the early days
When the Blacklegs rode in force;
When a feller was hung fer killin' a man,
And stealin' the man's best horse.
He swore that he was innocent
Tho' he knew with his life he must pay
For the crime of the man who wanted his land,
And the heart of the girl down the way.
They stood him up in a wagon box
Where a rope hung down from a tree;
But, before he died, his voice rang out,
"I'll git you...jist wait an' see."
The feller that framed him took over his land,
An' it wasn't long 'fore he moved in.
He seemed like a kind, respectable gent,
But was greedy clear up to his chin.
One day a farmer rode up to his door
An' shouted, "Yer barn is on fire."
It looked like it was a-burnin' down
With the flames gittin' higher and higher.
They ran fer water but when they got back
There was nuthin' new to be learned.
There wasn't a trace, nor the smell of smoke,
Nor a place where a fire had burned.
The horses were rarin', an' kickin' 'round,
An' a-wantin' to git outside;

An' the men heard the squeakin' of hinges
As the barn door opened wide.
Then unseen hands untied each horse,
An' they rared back from their stalls;
An' they never heard their owner,
Nor the farmer's frenzied calls.
But they tore down that country road,
An' never did come back,
An' there are those who still contend
They never left a track.
From then on so many things happened,
And the neighbors all stayed away;
And the owner went almost crazy,
An' he disappeared one day.
There is nothing left on the hill now
To tell of what used to be,
But sometimes the night winds whisper,
"…I'll git you…jist wait an' see."

CHILDREN'S SECTION

What's sadder than a cemetery? The children's section of a cemetery.

Yet it's surprising more cemeteries don't have them, considering the early mortality rate of children in Noble County and similar newly settled areas. One prime example of a children's cemetery can be found in Lake

An area of children's graves at Kendallville's Lake View Cemetery. *Emily Hunter.*

View Cemetery north of Kendallville, which spreads out along both sides of Riley Road.

In one corner, lined by the road and a border fence, is a section occupied almost entirely by the graves of children. It can be assumed that this is by design. The simple math of birth and death dates tells a heartbreaking story, often of newborns who lived only a few days.

We found no ghost stories from sections like this. They're not haunted—but haunting.

8
Rose Hill Cemetery

Rose Hill Cemetery's only real distinction is that it lies close to the geographic center of Noble County. It's not the biggest, fanciest, most isolated or (probably) spookiest graveyard in the County. Rose Hill is one of Noble County's older cemeteries though. Plus, from a ghost story standpoint, it has the advantage of actually being inside the town limits of Albion, rather than on the edge of a community or out in rural areas. That means there are more chances for people to see something…odd.

Ryan Castle, an Albion police officer, makes the cemetery part of his nightly patrol. That also makes him a regular visitor to spook central, as it were. We met Ryan just before midnight, during a full moon, in a cemetery where low-lying, dim solar lights illuminate tombstones here and there, between the black outlines of pine trees.

It's the perfect atmosphere for a ghostly conversation.

Two weeks before, at that very spot, Ryan spotted a patch of mist that seemed to dart with purpose up a hill, disregarding the wind. It headed in the general direction of a murdered man's tombstone, which we'll cover later.

A video he showed us was more hair-raising. He was with a newer officer, showing him the routine or perhaps testing the man's mental stamina, when they noticed a small pinwheel that was part of the decorations for one grave. The pinwheel was spinning madly, as pinwheels are designed to do. But it wasn't facing the wind.

In the video, the other officer blows some cigarette smoke toward the windmill to demonstrate that it was *not* being powered by the breeze. No

Rose Hill Cemetery in Albion has been the setting for more than one supernatural experience. *Mark Hunter.*

battery was involved. After a time, it stopped, much like a person's heart might have done on seeing it.

When Ryan Castle came by to look at the pinwheel on a later night, it was gone.

On another patrol, Ryan was startled to see someone lying along the side of a lane in the cemetery. The figure got up, moved toward a headstone and then disappeared. The grave was that of an infant, Harold C. Conrad, who was born in 1937 and passed away just two days later. Even sadder, the infant was buried in a section near the north edge of the area, named on the cemetery map "potters' field."

Potters' fields were areas set aside for the burials of poor or unknown people. The term dates to biblical times, when priests bought land once owned by clay pot makers for their burial grounds.

How little Harold ended up in the potters' field area isn't certain. His parents, Everett and Marion Conrad, are known and themselves buried in Ligonier's Oak Park Cemetery. They were in their twenties when little Harold passed away, and it's possible they couldn't afford a grave at the time—or maybe they were too grieved to deal with it.

So, if the figure that disappeared at the headstone was a ghost, whose was it? Surely it was not the spirit of a two-day-old. Maybe his parents were coming to visit. But can ghosts travel on their own? There are no hard and set rules on that subject.

At the same cemetery, Ryan also recorded orbs—either floating supernatural objects or motes of dust caught in the light, depending on who you ask. They appeared on one of the photos we took that night.

His curiosity raised, Ryan invested in a ghost hunting app for his phone. These apps use various means to detect the presence of spirits, like magnetic field fluctuations, and are controversial even within ghost hunting groups. If we understand the tech correctly, ghosts can sample distant radio signals with which to communicate, and Ryan did net a few words that way. Or perhaps it's the ghosts speaking directly.

We installed one of the apps, this one purporting to use what amounts to stick outlines to show where spirits stand or move around. According to it, someone—something—was sitting comfortably in a corner armchair in our living room. It hasn't spoken yet, and from where it sits, it can't see the TV.

One of the more interesting vaults at Rose Hill Cemetery was covered in vines for many years until it was uncovered to reveal a "B." *Mark Hunter.*

Murdered for His Money

The old joke about cemeteries is that people are dying to get in. What's seldom known is how the graveyard residents ended up in their plot. Often, of course, they died of natural causes or in accidents. Other times, they meet a more sinister end, like the one that led to this inscription on a monument in Rose Hill Cemetery:

> *Adam Hoffman*
> *Born Jan 13, 1816*
> *Murdered at his home for his money on the night of Oct. 15, 1897.*

It's safe to say there must be a story behind that. But the story begins not on the night of his death, but in 1890.

Adam Hoffman was an Albion merchant who rented housing to tenants on various farms in the area. He was working on one of those farms when a stranger approached him and called him by name. The stranger was an Indian Agent from out west. (An Indian Agent was someone authorized to deal with Natives on behalf of the United States government.) Now, he was searching for a large amount of gold buried by the Natives forty years previously in the Albion area.

Or so he said.

But the man's story was convincing. That would have been right around the time the last of the tribes were removed from Noble County, and maybe the gold was too much to carry on the long trip. The agent even had one of the Natives with him to find the location (although Hoffman never saw that other person). Hoffman followed the man into the nearby woods, where "X" proverbially marked the spot. There, Hoffman started to dig in unbroken ground until he struck a root, which required an axe to remove it.

Hoffman retrieved an axe, and when he returned, a little more digging revealed, sure enough, a gold brick, weighing around fifty pounds. According to the *Kendallville Standard* newspaper, the Indian Agent said the $14,500 bar was one of fifteen buried nearby.

As you might imagine, Adam Hoffman was pretty excited at this point, especially after the agent promised to divide the riches into thirds: one for him, one for Hoffman and one for their Native guide. Or Hoffman could buy the Natives share for just $1,000.

Hoffman, nobody's fool, demanded proof that the gold was real. So, the Indian Agent broke off a small piece—or more likely sneaked it out of his

Adam Hoffman's Albion gravestone makes his fate clear, but the identity of his killer has never been discovered. *Emily Hunter.*

pocket—and the men had it tested by J.P. Chapman, a druggist in Rome City. The nugget was, of course, pure gold.

Although the rest of the story was not.

The Indian Agent fled with his $1,000 on the Lake Shore train and jumped off somewhere between stops. His companion Native never appeared at all, and, of course, neither did the gold.

How much this story is related to Hoffman's death is uncertain. Certainly, he was wealthy by the standards of the day, but did someone also believe the gold could have been real? Maybe they were just after a more typical loot when they appeared at his house late on October 15, 1897, seven years later.

Hoffman was eighty-one at this point, so the thirteen-year-old son of one of his renters, young Charles Holey, stayed with him many nights to help with chores. On October 15, 1897, Charles was awakened by noises from Hoffman's room. Intruders then appeared and tied Charles to his bed.

They also gagged him—although you'd think their threats to be silent or else would suffice.

Soon, Charles heard the burglars ransacking the house and threatening to kill Adam Hoffman unless he gave them the location of his hidden money. That pretty much settles the question of motive.

After the robbers disappeared, Charles was able to free himself, at which point, he found Hoffman tied to his own bed—and quite dead.

When the town was finally alerted, a large crowd surrounded the house, which unfortunately kept the summoned bloodhounds from being able to find a scent. The suspects escaped—with about $1.50.

Could Adam Hoffman's spirit still be wandering the town or at least his burial location in Rose Hill Cemetery? Well, there are precious few murder victims buried in Noble County, thankfully. There are plenty of reports of possible paranormal activity in Rose Hill Cemetery. Perhaps one day, investigators will narrow the hauntings there down to Adam Hoffman. Or perhaps, like his killers, Hoffman will never get the blame.

9

Bakertown General Scare

Jefferson Township's Bakertown, originally called Baker's Corners, was established in 1854, when George Baker purchased eighty acres of land there. One piece of that was sold to Uriah Franks, who built not only his own home but also the Bakertown General Store. It even held the post office—oddly called the Stanley Post Office—for a few years. There was a blacksmith in town and, not far away, a sawmill.

But eventually, the town went the way of so many small villages built for the horse-drawn travel times: it slowly faded away. The store stopped operations around 1940. Most of what's left today consists of farm buildings, a T-intersection and the still-standing Bakertown Store, now a private residence. Bakertown became a ghost town—in more ways than one.

"The whole area around there is spooked out," explained Lachlan MacCallum. "Several of my neighbors and family members have seen a man in a dark robe, large-brimmed hat and empty eye sockets. We believe him to have been a Jesuit and call him The Priest."

It may seem like a character from a horror movie, but there have been numerous sightings. The Jesuits, an order of Roman Catholic priests, accompanied early European explorers as they came through the area. Back then, travel was often done over water, and a tributary to the Elkhart River (now called Summers Ditch) runs nearby.

The story goes that a French priest vanished along the Elkhart River after the French and Indian War, when some Natives turned against the losing French side. This particular priest had a stash of money with him, according to a student who attended Xavier College, a Jesuit Catholic school.

The Bakertown General Store was typical of small village businesses, but perhaps no others were so haunted. *Grace Leatherman Collection.*

One would wonder why a priest traveling in the primeval swamps of Indiana would have a lot of cash. Payroll?

So, instead of drowning or dying of disease, this priest was murdered for his valuables. It could very well be that the Natives took his remains up the stream to the area that would become Bakertown to ensure his body wouldn't be discovered.

This would certainly be enough to upset any man of the cloth.

Lachlan McCallum related stories of the priest being seen by his family members, as well as neighbors. One woman looked up while cleaning her car in the garage and saw a man dressed as a Jesuit only feet away. Another sighting occurred during a barn raising. Perhaps the buildings stood a bit too close to The Priest's final resting place—not that he's doing much resting.

As if all of that wasn't enough, it's said a woman who had been gored to death by a bull sometimes appears in a nearby field—the same field, one would presume, where she died.

It could be that story is related to another that involved the Bakertown Store. Linda Hatfield lived there during the 1960s and said she would have weird feelings about an attached part of the store where the family didn't live. Other than that, nothing unusual happened—until she moved away.

That's when she started having dreams about being in the converted store and trying to climb upstairs but being stopped by a woman with flowing hair and a long gown. She had the dream for years and tried to shake it off; then she finally confided in her oldest daughter.

It turned out that her daughter had experienced the exact same dream.

Oddly, once they told each other about the dream, neither of them ever suffered through it again.

10

There's No Business Like Ghost Business

Before movie theaters came along, communities had opera houses. Yes, sometimes operas were performed there, but these venues were used for just about all forms of entertainment or public service. Albion's opera house boasted, at various times, roller skating, school graduations, basketball games, political rallies, plays and motion picture showings.

In 1890, the Spencer Opera House went up on Main Street in Kendallville. It could seat about 750 and hosted a variety of shows, including vaudeville acts. After World War I, it was refurbished as a theater, and in 1929, the Hudson family bought it and renamed it The Strand. It was, by all accounts, a great place to go and work.

And if you love where you work, why leave? Ever?

The Strand is still there; according to some people, so is its legendary (and deceased) former manager Cleon Point. But hold on to your popcorn, because here's a plot twist: The Strand Theater might have not one but three ghosts.

Cleon Point worked at The Strand mostly as manager from 1946 to 1979. He was much beloved and much feared, depending on whether you were a kid acting up in his theater. Some say he's still seen patrolling the aisles and keeping an eye on things, but Mr. Point doesn't directly factor into most of the hauntings reported there.

The theater's second spirit is a woman who walked into the theater one day and never came out. How we know she never came out isn't clear, but if Cleon Point was on duty at the time, he would no doubt have been watching

Built in 1890, The Strand would be Noble County's most haunted movie theater if it wasn't the only movie theater still standing. *Mark Hunter.*

for stragglers. Exactly what happened to her is also not clear, but a ghostly white apparition has supposedly been seen by residents living in the building walking through third floor walls.

There's just one problem: there are no residents living in The Strand building. And there's no third floor.

Most likely, the story is mixing up Kendallville's Strand with another Strand Theater, such as the one in Angola that's also supposed to be haunted.

Back to the Kendallville Strand. There's little doubt that at one time in its long history, The Strand featured a pipe organ, something to accompany both live acts and silent movies back in the day. This might be why at least one person said they heard organ music coming from the building—although this occurred after the turn of this century, decades after a physical organ might have been in place in the theater.

Then there's the ghostly figure of a man who can be seen in the projection room window, watching people in the theater down below. When someone looks up, it's said he ducks down from view.

This spirit is said to be a former owner who ended his own life in, yes, the projection room.

At first glance, there's an obvious explanation: the projection room is where the projectionist works, and it's hard to imagine he didn't look out the window. If, in the old days, you've ever yelled, "Focus! Focus!" he's the man you were yelling at.

At second glance, there are only so many ways to get to a projection room. The story goes that an employee, while cleaning in The Strand, had her kids with her, and they spotted a man at the top of the stairs that led to the balcony. They described the man to another worker, who, a few days later, saw the same man in the projection room. They ran up the stairs, the only way to get to that room.

The projection room was empty.

The male worker later encountered someone who came to buy the theater, someone who looked much like the mysterious figure. He discovered the visitor was the son of a former owner, who did, indeed, end his own life in that room.

There have been more sightings of this particular figure in other areas of the theater, but there are problems with the story.

First, no report of a death by suicide occurring at The Strand can be substantiated. It's something that very likely would have made both the news and the rumor mill of the time.

No reports could be found of a son buying The Strand after his father died, although there have been "family" ownerships, including ownership by the Deardorfs, the Flynns and the Hudsons.

As for the authors of this book, one of us (Mark) has indeed seen a figure in the projection room window and even saw that figure duck away. When you're a kid and see something like that, you just turn back and wait for *King Kong vs. Godzilla* to start. Mark has only ever been disturbed by fellow living patrons during a movie.

11
Haunt for Teacher

When you're a student, you may want your school to be haunted. Anything to break the monotony, right? It worked for Buffy, the vampire slayer.

That's exactly why any tales of haunted schools should be considered with caution. Sure, it could be spirits—or it could be bored or mischievous students trying to scare each other.

Tales of ghosts at East Noble High School, located on the south side of Kendallville, have gone around for years. The complex was built in 1966, after some surrounding homes were removed, reportedly through eminent domain.

One of the residents who lost his home was an angry man named Otto, who vowed he'd have his revenge against the school. How and when Otto passed away isn't certain, but apparently, even death didn't cool his anger.

Otto, dressed in old-style dark trousers and a white jacket, can be seen standing at the entrance to the East Noble High School main gym. He's also been known to watch students from the gym bleachers and even walk beside students before suddenly disappearing. Maybe his house stood where the gym now is. Or maybe he liked gym class, which seems less likely.

But Otto wasn't the first ghost to roam around the property. A janitor reportedly spotted a little girl in the cafeteria, who then disappeared as he watched. A little girl? In a high school?

But the high school was built partially on the previous location of Kendallville's Southside Elementary School.

Kendallville Central High School looked like it should be haunted, but its 1966 replacement is the one collecting ghosts. *Noble County Historical Society.*

Often, a tale of someone dying in an unusual place can't be substantiated, but in the case of East Noble High School, a particularly tragic tale is true.

A female student died in a science room, apparently part of an experiment gone wrong. It's said that night shift janitors have since heard the TV in that room turn on by itself, often to MTV.

A report of an explosion or chemical leak leading to a death in the building couldn't be found in local news media, but we were surprised to learn that it did happen.

Wendy Lynne Rhoades was the daughter of much-loved educator Gene Rhodes. She was reportedly working on experiments in the lab attached to the school's biology room when she was overcome, possibly by carbon monoxide.

To make the tragedy even worse, when it happened in 1979, Wendy's father, Gene, was the East Noble High School principal, and her mother, Virginia Rhoades, taught chemistry and biology at the school. It's hard to imagine they could continue teaching in the same place, but from what we've learned about Gene and Virginia Rhoades, they were people of great dedication and caring. East Noble was lucky to have them.

Perhaps that explains why Wendy continues to occupy the place her parents loved, and there's no indication she ever tried to scare anyone. If she wanted to watch MTV from back when it played actual music, who could blame her?

Meanwhile, the new East Noble Middle School could very well have gotten a head start in being haunted. Kay Mapes Mason told us of an old farmhouse on Drake Road in Kendallville, and according to the story she heard, a child may have been hit by a vehicle on Drake Road, and then she haunted the house.

In 2018, the old home was torn down and replaced by the East Noble Middle School. It could have easily been one of those cases of "building on a graveyard" hauntings, but luckily, the school seems to have escaped that curse—at least until some imaginative young student tells the story.

12

Haunted Hospitals, Funeral Homes and the Noble County Asylum

At the exact center of Noble County—or, at least, what was the exact center before a swamp-isolated slice of the county's southwest corner was turned over to Whitley County—stands the Noble County Courthouse. Built in 1887 in a Richardsonian Romanesque style, the courthouse was constructed in the same place where two previous courthouses stood. The first was brought down by a suspected arson fire that came close to killing several people and burning down the town of Albion. The second—well, the second just didn't hold up and had to be replaced. There's no record of someone dying inside any of the buildings, despite many close calls, but it was the starting point of one of the more famous deaths from Noble County's earlier history.

On September 25, 1908, acrobat Madame La Fere was asked to do her famous "slide for life" in Albion. Her real name was Ethel Skiver, of West Unity, Ohio, and she traveled across the country doing various tricks to show off her skills. Hanging by her hair, Madame La Fere would slide down a wire from the courthouse tower, across Orange Street, to an alley east of the courthouse square.

But this time, the cable snapped.

In front of the horrified crowd, La Fere fell seventy-five feet onto Orange Street. Bystanders took her to the Good Hope Hospital, just a block away, where she later died.

This means that when one of the authors (Mark) later lived in the former hospital, he may have been sleeping in the same patient room where Ethel Skiver and an unknown number of other people passed away.

One of the most haunting images in Noble County history shows Madame Le Fere's "Slide for Life," which ended tragically on another run. *Noble County Historical Society.*

The good news for our peace of mind is that when Mark lived in the building, he had no idea it had been the Good Hope Hospital. So, the occasional strange creak or bump that could be heard upstairs was not the power of suggestion. We attribute it to a building settling into its old age. Maybe that was it.

Maybe it wasn't.

A Luckey Tunnel

Small hospitals sprouted up all over early Noble County, and one had its own connection with the Noble County Courthouse: both buildings contained hidden tunnels. At the courthouse, a tunnel ran south to a building on Hazel Street, where steam was generated to heat the courthouse during winter. Much of the tunnel was filled in when the street between them was replaced. We had a chance to go down into it before we saw the size of the spiders.

The Luckey Hospital stood and still stands in Wolf Lake at the intersection of State Road 109 and U.S. Highway 33, famously called the Lincoln

Highway. According to local resident Annie Sheets, the now-boarded-up tunnel led from the hospital's basement to a home nearby.

That was the home of Dr. James Luckey, who had the tunnel built for him to travel to and from the hospital. After Dr. Luckey's death in 1938, the second floor of his home was converted to nurses' quarters, allowing them to utilize the tunnel to avoid adverse weather. Even in a small-town, safety was also a reasonable precaution, considering that at the time, streetlights were likely few and far between in such places.

It does make one wonder how many other old tunnels still exist across the country.

One also wonders if any of the nurses stayed in what was once the Wolf Lake Hotel, a building that still stands across U.S. Highway 33 from the Luckey Hospital. The hotel is now a home, and at least one resident says they experienced odd goings-on while there. Another says the hospital itself has had reports of hauntings.

Dr. Luckey was born at the close of the Civil War. He got his medical degree in 1892 from what became the Indiana University School of Medicine and returned to Wolf Lake around 1893. He practiced out of his home and then a small wood-frame building. In 1928, the building was torn

The Luckey Hospital was named after its founder and has the good luck to still be standing after its construction in 1929. *Mark Hunter*.

down, and construction began on what would become the Luckey Hospital, with a new residence beside it.

The Luckey Hospital gained a reputation for excellence, and patients were referred to it from across the area. But as more modern hospitals were built in other communities, Luckey Hospital became obsolete. After its closure in 1959, it became a nursing home for a time and then a museum. Now, it stands as an apartment building, although Dr. Luckey's residence was demolished.

All this came very close to never happening. Dr. Luckey, a popular physician by all accounts, made house calls, as all doctors did at the time. But in 1918, while visiting a Wolf Lake store, he encountered someone who apparently didn't care for him—and demonstrated that discontent with a knife.

The gravely injured Dr. Luckey determined he wouldn't survive a car ride and instead *walked* several blocks to his home, where other doctors cared for him. Cars were unreliable back then, as were the roads they traveled. Maybe this experience helped lead him to founding the hospital.

It also should be noted that Dr. Luckey once had to be treated for injuries he received from a bear—*his own* bear.

FUNERAL ARRANGEMENTS

An uncle of one of the authors (Emily) directed a funeral home in Missouri and had his residence in the same building. Only a door separated the home from the parlor. Emily's first experience with the building came when she hid in the basement, where it's presumed the mortuary was, during a tornado warning.

Funeral homes are a natural magnet for ghost stories, of course. A historic building in Cromwell, believed to be the 1910 Forrest Henney Funeral Home, has some spooky tales behind it. If it's the same funeral home—and there weren't that many in Cromwell—it's since been renovated into a home. It's possible the occupants don't even know its former occupation, and maybe that's for the best.

One alleged funeral home haunting happened just over the Noble County line. Screams can supposedly be heard coming from the basement of the funeral home in Wolcottville. Maybe a living person stubbed their toe? A separate witness also had odd experiences in the building.

In any case, Wolcottville straddles the Noble/LaGrange County line, and that funeral home is a stone's throw into LaGrange County, which gives us an excellent excuse to never go into that basement.

THE POOR HOUSE OF MANY NAMES

Hospitals and retirement homes might be expected to hold ghosts, as could asylums of various sorts. One place in Noble County has been all three and is reported to be very much haunted.

In fact, the Noble County Infirmary went by several names over the years, and more than one was official. Constructed in 1871, the building still stands on County Road 100 West, about a mile or two northwest of Albion.

Poor houses were common at the time, but this one was also called the Poor Farm, along with its more official name. The location, which replaced a former infirmary on another property that had been donated eleven years before, featured 160 acres of land along with farm buildings. The occupants who weren't too elderly or ill worked the farm, raising their own food.

It even had its own graveyard.

Residents of the Noble County Poor Farm were expected, if they were able, to help produce their own food. *Noble County Historical Society.*

Many of the County Farm Cemetery graves were lost to time until volunteers rehabilitated the area. *Emily Hunter.*

The building later became a nursing home and now holds apartments. It still has attention-grabbing fire escape slides along either side—an attraction for kids who lived there. The graveyard down the road is now called the Wright Cemetery, but a portion of it to the east remains known as the County Home Cemetery and holds the graves of the unfortunate residents who passed away there.

The ornate brick building *looks* like it must be haunted. According to some local residents it is, but details are lacking.

Lori Wilson Gagen of Albion had an experience there that helps tell the story.

When the owner at the time was on vacation in 2012, Lori and her friends got permission to ghost hunt there while they house sat in the old building. At about 10:00 p.m., they shut off the lights, as seems to be traditional with ghost hunters (we would have left them on), and split up: three women on the second floor, three men in the basement.

The experience seemed anticlimactic. Despite the age of the building, the number of people who lived and died there and even the existence of cells in the basement, they saw and heard no sign of supernatural activity. (The cells were apparently for residents suffering from mental conditions or possibly Alzheimer's—a horrifying prospect today that was normal back then.)

The group left a digital recorder running the whole time so they could listen for what ghost hunters call EVPs, or electronic voice phenomenon. They didn't catch anything of interest.

Or so they thought.

Around midnight, Lori got a hysterical phone call from one of the other women, who had stayed up and listened to the entire recording. Most of it was just the women talking to each other, but as they announced their intention to leave the second floor, a clear voice of a female child said, "I'm so bored."

You'd be bored, too, if you were stuck in one building for decades.

Later, Lori played us the recording. It was clearly understood and definitely not from one of the people exploring the place.

At that time, nobody lived upstairs, but later, someone moved into one of the apartments and related another story to Lori. The night he moved in, he heard footprints coming down the hall to his bedroom door. He thought

Although its occupants no longer work the land around it, the Noble County Poor House still stands, now divided into apartments. *Mark Hunter.*

it was a living human, but when someone just stood by the door, shuffling around, he opened it to see who his visitor was.

As you've already guessed, there was no one there.

As we walked around the County Home Cemetery late one autumn afternoon, we had to wonder: Why *wouldn't* the location be haunted? You would think at least some of its residents would be dissatisfied with their lives in one way or another.

But the current occupants don't seem to be bothered, so maybe it's better not to look too closely.

13

Libraries and Friendly Ghosts

Libraries are especially popular among certain people, such as writers, readers and, of course, librarians. Ghosts are perfectly welcome there—as long as they maintain silence in the library.

The Cromwell branch of the Noble County Public Library (NCPL) is located on a historic business block and was expanded to include the old Cromwell Opera House into its operations. Moving into an old anything is a red flag when it comes to ghosts.

The expansion included the installation of an elevator to access an upper floor, something elevators excel at. But according to the NCPL's Jennifer Steffey, the elevator immediately developed problems.

"Among other things, it would randomly go upstairs with no one there, so Janet [another employee] just said it must be 'Tillie' the ghost. An elevator inspector…said that according to his counts, there had been over one million passes on the elevator, which seems pretty implausible."

While it's true elevators are statistically the safest way to travel—even when haunted—that does seem like a high number for a community library. In addition to that, according to Jennifer, "He [the inspector] got pretty spooked when Janet casually mentioned Tillie."

Why the name Tillie? Well, why not?

A few years later, a family rented the opera house for a wedding reception. "The elevator didn't work," reported Jennifer, "the air conditioning was iffy, and the wedding cake fell over when nobody was there. Just very weird stuff."

When the Cromwell branch of the Noble County Public Library moved in, at least one previous occupant of the building stuck around. *Mark Hunter.*

When the same family had another event a few months later, family members walked into the opera house and called out, "Tillie, you can come to the party—we would love to have you here!" Which was very nice of them. The second time, there were no issues.

Next came a class reunion, and one of the returning classmates happened to be a psychic. She soon left, saying the opera house gave her a headache because of the energy there.

Jennifer said that a few days later, the woman returned to the library and told the staff they had a ghost there named Violet. Not only that, but a man and a boy also seemed to be there, although the psychic could not give names for them.

Finally, the psychic reported, "She doesn't mind being called Tillie but does prefer Violet."

Why so much ghost activity at this particular library? Well, according to the library's Tabitha Kethcart, that business block used to contain a morgue.

"I do believe the morgue was next door at the Hobby Shop," Tabitha said. "At least that's what it looks like from the research." Just to make it clear, the Hobby Shop was not there at the same time as the morgue.

In addition to that, the block was among fourteen businesses that burned down on the night of Halloween 1909. Certainly, a disaster like that could rouse restless spirits. The fire itself might seem like just a scary story, but it really happened—we scared up some photos of the aftermath.

Whether any of that is connected can't be determined. Tabitha was part of a ghost walk, during which two teenagers said they saw a ghost move across a closet in the old opera house area. In any case, Violet—or Tillie, if you prefer—seems perfectly harmless...as long as she gets an invite to the party.

CARNEGIE HAUNT

In 1890, E.B. Spencer built a reading room in Kendallville, an early library effort that sadly lasted only a year. Its story is mostly interesting to us because Spencer also built the Spencer Opera House, now the haunted Strand Theater not far away.

Another attempt began in 1902, and by 1911, an effort by the citizens led to books being collected in the basement of the Kendallville School. Finally, in 1914, with a site donated by the Jacobs family and an Andrew Carnegie Foundation grant, a true library went into service at Grant and Rush Streets. More Carnegie Libraries were constructed in Indiana than in any other state.

The one in Kendallville is haunted, of course.

Now, the former Kendallville Library is privately owned after it was replaced in 1968. Since then, it's had some odd reports. A witness says the old wooden doors in the bathroom open and close when no one else is in the building, which might make witnesses need to use that very room. After the library moved to a larger location in 1968 (at the location of a Civil War training camp), a series of private businesses moved into the old building, including an attorney's office, an architecture firm, a vintage clothing store and an art gallery. How many of those occupants got scared near the bathroom isn't known. Perhaps the spirits, being book lovers, moved with the library.

Another beautiful Carnegie library, the first purpose-built library in Noble County stands in Ligonier. It's served the community continuously since

One of many Carnegie Libraries, the Kendallville facility was built in 1913–14. How long it's been haunted isn't so certain. *Mike Mapes collection.*

Ligonier's Carnegie Library, built in 1908, is still serving the community. *Mark Hunter.*

1908 and is watched over by more or less friendly spirits—more because the staff likes having their ghost around and less because the spirit's appearance was, like so many hauntings, brought on by tragedy.

The story goes that long ago, a librarian in Ligonier was asked to step down from her position. Why she did this, we don't know; the position of a librarian is one that becomes not just a job but also a vocation and a love. Her heart broken, the librarian ended her own life.

Being unable to find any record of such a death involving the Ligonier Library, we sincerely hope it didn't happen that way. And since the spirit there seems more playful than upset, we're inclined to think there was some embellishing going on.

In 2007, the Ligonier Public Library received a late-night visit by an organization called Fort Wayne Ghost Trackers, following up on numerous reports of supernatural happenings. Ghosts have been seen, their footsteps heard, and from time to time, they've moved objects and even thrown books off the shelves. Still, none of the staff has ever been harmed, and they maintain their ghost is the friendly sort.

The Ghost Trackers spent hours in the building and came back with photos of mysterious orbs and records of sudden changes in temperature far out of line, even for an older building. When they asked questions out loud, they noticed large swings in local electromagnetic fields. Their conclusion: the Ligonier Public Library is haunted.

Nobody was inclined to disagree, and they hope the building will stand and be haunted for years to come.

Library Connections

We were disappointed to discover no reports of supernatural activity from the Kendallville Public Library's current main branch in Kendallville. The library was built in the footprints of Lakeside Hospital, later McCray Memorial Hospital, so life and death has occurred there since 1912. It's also where one of us (Mark) and so many other people were born—and many others died.

Mark wants to eventually haunt the Noble County Public Library's main branch in Albion—because it's a library. But he spent most of his library time at that place's original location, a Carnegie building on the Noble County Courthouse square. That location is now part of the Noble County Government Annex, where Mark works as a 911 dispatcher.

Lakeside Hospital in Kendallville became McCray Memorial Hospital before it was replaced in 2007 by a new Kendallville Public Library. *Mike Mapes collection.*

In a way, that completes a circle. The library location, now a government facility, is the site of Albion's first Noble County Jail. (The first county jail was located a few miles west in Augusta when it was the county seat.)

The first jail in Albion was a basic handmade log structure set up inside a frame building. It was the setting of at least one escape by a suspect named Bill Hill in the 1850s, and at least one witness insisted it was inferior to the Augusta jail.

14
Show Me the Way to Kneipp Sanitarium

Many years ago, one of us (Mark) attended a fire department tour of a location in Rome City, which had changed ownership and planned to open again. Snow was falling hard as Mark wandered into the basement and discovered a secret door.

OK, it wasn't really a secret. But it was an old wooden door with no signs on it that led into the wall, so naturally, he opened it and walked in. A tunnel went on for some distance, and he got snowed on once from a grate far above. At the end was a small grotto with spring water flowing from it. We wish he'd had a camera back then, since he visited only once.

But he remembers getting a chill, as if he was the first to discover a place that had some kind of enchantment—or, you know, ghosts.

Kneipp Springs, Kneipp Sanatorium, Kneipp Sanitarium, Kneipp Springs Health Spa, The Way College or the part that's now Sylvan Cellars Event Center and Tasting Room—whatever the place is called, this Rome City location seems overwhelmingly large and complex, at least to rural Indiana people who aren't used to such a thing. It's changed a lot over the years and was once close to a railroad station. Between the railroad and the recreational areas around nearby Sylvan Lake, the place was especially busy in the summer.

Is it haunted? You bet.

In fact, it's a battlefield in the war of good versus evil.

The story starts not in Rome City but with a German priest named Sebastian Kneipp, who was said to cure his tuberculosis by swimming several

Only an overhead view of the Kneipp Sanitarium property can truly show the scope of the operation. *Mike Mapes collection.*

times a week in the freezing waters of the Danube River. For you classical music fans, there's a "Blue Danube" joke in there somewhere.

Kneipp lived to be seventy-six in the 1800s, so who's to argue?

Meanwhile, in 1882, F.M. Buker built a three-story structure at Northport, now a ghost town just north of Rome City. He grew celery, established a trout hatchery, discovered mineral springs and found out there was no money in farming celery. That's when Dr. W.C. Geiemann, a student of Kneipp's methods, acquired the property and established Kneipp Sanitarium in 1895.

It had accommodations for ten guests. The place prospered, and by 1920, its eighty acres were occupied with over twenty buildings surrounded by walks and gardens, not to mention the twelve springs that flowed south of the main building; 250 guests could be treated at the same time, and the employees worked a large farm.

In 1901, The Sisters of the Precious Blood began running the operation. They faced many challenges, but the one that might most interest us is that, when State Road 9 was run right through the property in 1936, they had to move a cemetery that had been there since 1914.

It seems like moving cemeteries never ends well.

It was the sisters who, for some reason, decided to build a parking lot over the original spring. They dug a tunnel to the spring, the same tunnel Mark

The Rome City Railroad Depot brought people from around the country to the Kneipp Sanitarium, the town and Sylvan Lake. *Mike Mapes Collection.*

stumbled across many years later. The water is still available to passers-by via a three-spigot fount, installed in 2022 ten feet above the spring.

We sampled the spring water and found it refreshing—but without a supernatural oomph.

In 1966, Kneipp Springs added a licensed nursing unit, but in 1976, facing declining income, the property was sold. It was run for a time by The Way College of Biblical Research, a religious organization that was rumored to be a type of cult. It reportedly stripped the complex of its Catholic heritage, even boarding up the stained-glass windows of the chapel, before moving out in 1999.

So, Kneipp Springs had a complicated history and still does, with a large barn on the property now home to the Sylvan Cellars Event and Tasting Room. The main building and its surroundings include, among other things, a chapel, group tour spots, the artesian spring itself and, of course, a shrine to Our Lady, Patroness of America. The latter is where the battle between good and evil comes in.

On September 25, 1956, Precious Blood Sister Mildred Mary Ephrem Neuzil felt a presence as she prayed in the chapel. The next day, she saw it—or rather, it saw her. It was the Virgin Mary. This probably didn't come as a surprise to Sister Mildred, who'd had visions of The Virgin for eighteen years, mostly at a previous post in Ohio.

But it was in the Kneipp Springs Chapel that Mary told Mildred her new name: Our Lady of America.

Mary wanted the United States to be a country dedicated to purity, and we think it's safe to assume she was disappointed. Still, a beautiful, nine-foot-tall statue of the Patroness of America now stands at the site. Strange apparitions are seen at Kneipp Springs from time to time.

Are they good apparitions or bad? Probably both.

Jennifer James and Jill Stanley, mystics and paranormal investigators, declared in their *Common Mystics* podcast that Kneipp Springs is one of the most haunted locations they've ever happened upon. They stumbled across the property (not by accident, they believe) at a time between when The Way had left and the buildings were rehabilitated, so it had the spooky feel of an abandoned place.

Creepy is a word they used a lot when describing the location, and for them, the main building put out a lot of energy. Mark felt this himself during his tour of the complex years prior but put it down to how much he likes exploring big buildings.

Overcome with the feeling they were being watched, the podcasters retreated from the building and stumbled across the Grotto to the Blessed Mother, which had been there, by then, for many years. It gave them comfort

The Kneipp Springs main building remains one of the largest and most impressive structures in the area. *Mike Mapes collection.*

but also a sense that good energies from there were opposing bad energies from the building.

Later, the ladies say they found two cases of deaths by suicide that had occurred on the property, but we were unable to substantiate these claims. They also said Sister Mildred tried to avoid being assigned to the sanitarium and felt a terrible sense of evil there before The Virgin came to her. This is not in Mildred's diary, so we can't substantiate that claim, either.

One other detail from the *Common Mystics* podcast: Jennifer and Jill say the Natives of the area, before being driven out of Noble County, revered the springs in Northport as holy ground. They also point out—and this is something we were able to confirm—pre-Native Mound Builders left mounds in the Rome City area.

Their conclusion is that the Kneipp Springs property is indeed haunted. That's also the conclusion of Albion Police Officer Ryan Castle, who responded with two other officers when they received a report of two suspects breaking into the empty building. As they were clearing the rooms they heard a thud in the hallway. In addition, a door shut with no one near it, and a two-by-four board suddenly fell over.

When they heard a moan coming from the attic area, once a dorm for people who stayed at Kneipp Springs, they ran upstairs to catch whoever was running around inside.

No one was there.

Incidentally, it's said that a woman who drowned herself on the property haunts that floor.

This wasn't Ryan's first encounter with the supernatural. The fact that he and the others stayed to clear the entire building means he was inside much longer than we would have been.

15

Religious Institutions and the Haunted Church That Wasn't

As with tales of haunted schools, reports of haunted churches should often be taken with a grain of salt—or, as previously suggested, a circle of salt.

Just as some people don't like schools—or, at least, want to get out of the Big Test—others don't like religion. When someone doesn't like something, the next step is to say things about it to turn others away, too. After all, the thinking may go: If a religious facility isn't powerful enough to kick out resident ghosts, how good could it be?

So, we start with an intriguing and scary haunting that just isn't. This church is located near Riley and Mitchell Streets in Kendallville, and in this book, it will not be named, although we're confident no one who reads it would be low enough to start more rumors. In any case, professional investigators have declared this a zero-ghost zone.

In a way, that's too bad, because if the story was true, it would make for an awesome scary movie. In fact, everything scary that's ever appeared in a ghost story appears here, which is, by itself, a warning sign of a hoax.

For instance, people's faces are said to be seen in mirrors—and not the faces of the people looking into those mirrors. Footsteps can be heard on the stairs, cold and warm spots are felt and invisible "things" touch unwary worshippers. Scratching can be heard on the walls, with marks left behind. Tall, dark figures can not only move chairs, but they also sometimes throw them. People have reported being chased out and having cuts appear on their arms and legs or bruises on their abdomens. A dark shadow in a kitchen chased people upstairs and then disappeared.

All of that? In one place? Why hasn't a book been written? Why has no one investigated?

The answer to that last one is easy: someone did.

The Northeast Indiana Paranormal Investigators, shortened to NEIPIS for obvious reasons, came to the church's rescue and spent eighty hours investigating the facility. Now, remember, these are people who want to believe. They also want their beliefs to be backed up by evidence, but they found none at this Kendallville church. Lori Fuelling, one of the founders of the group (which now appears to be defunct), noted that every time she got the building removed from lists of haunted places, it was listed again within a week—apparently by the person who started the story to begin with.

This ghost story reportedly started with a former parishioner who was asked to leave the church. The rest of the details we don't know, but for some people, revenge is a favorite pastime.

Some people hate churches or any religious organization. That tempts us toward disbelief when it comes to two other reports of church hauntings, especially since they're located only blocks from the last one.

In fact, we added the Restoration Lutheran Church mostly as a way to help it out. The alleged stories are all too familiar: ghostly footsteps on the stairs, faces in mirrors, scratching sounds, hot and cold spots. That last experience would almost be expected in a building that old and large. Alleged witnesses also said tall, dark figures have been seen and have even thrown furniture at people.

It all sounds very familiar, doesn't it? It's so familiar that we don't believe it, especially since the building stays busy as a community center. Either someone is confusing the two churches, or someone wants to harass them both.

So, if this part seems less like a ghost story and more like promotion of the Apple Tree Center and its gifts to the community, like preschool services, meals and other activities—oh, well.

Our feelings are similar about the IGA—excuse us, the Destiny Family of Faith Church—just down Riley Street (And across from Jim's Pizza—yum!). When Mark was a child, he used to play in that neighborhood, and at the time, the building was an IGA grocery store. Later, with an influx of Hispanic families to the area, it became a Mexican food store, but now, it serves proudly as a church.

The allegations are familiar: footsteps, scratching noises, cold spots and tall, dark apparitions. Some witnesses claimed they were touched by an unseen force or saw objects moving by themselves.

The congregation of Restoration Lutheran Church isn't afraid of ghosts—because it doesn't have any. *Mark Hunter*.

Once an IGA grocery store, the building is now the Destiny Family of Faith Church, serving its community in a different way. *Mark Hunter*.

We consider ourselves open-minded, or we wouldn't have tackled this book to begin with. However, it's hard to imagine the leadership of a church couldn't drive out a few playful spirits—or at least get them to sit quietly in the back pew. In the case of the Destiny Family of Faith Church, we suspect that if anyone is haunting it, it's a shopper from the '70s who keeled over at the rising cost of food.

A similar story comes from the Blessed Sacrament Church on the south side of Albion. Albion Officer Ryan Castle, who's developed a nose for strange events, found an open door at that location while on patrol one night. Castle and another officer found that, while the chapel door was still locked, the door to the community center was open. They cleared the building, and once they were sure no one was inside, they returned to find the door they'd entered shut and secured, locking them in.

Why is that story similar to the one from the Destiny Family of Faith Church? Because the Blessed Sacrament community center was also, like the Kendallville house of worship, originally an IGA grocery store.

16

Haunted Kendallville

Is it possible that an entire town could be haunted? After all, Noble County is full of ghost towns. However, that holds a different meaning in this case; Kendallville is the largest community in the county, not a fading crossroads.

Noah Shepherd's experience may indicate that Kendallville is practically a phantom factory, or maybe he himself is a ghost magnet, something we're sure he'd prefer was not the case.

Noah's earliest ghostly memory dates to when he was four or five years old, living in a Williams Street house that was built in the latter half of the nineteenth century. He describes seeing a toddler in the kitchen and offering them some Cheerios. Dressed in an old-fashioned, rag-like diaper, the child had curly hair and pale, slightly grey skin. He offered the apparition toys, not realizing it was an apparition, but "the boy would never respond to my callings."

It turned out that when Noah's older brother was around the same age, he would ask their mother who the boy was and where he came from. "I'm sure at the time my mom's heart dropped to her stomach when she had two out of four children say they'd seen the same apparition."

Noah said he never felt alone in any room in the house, but the scariest experience came one day when he was alone playing and heard that same brother's bedroom doorknob jiggle. He didn't give it a thought at first—other than that his brother might be pranking him—but when the handle kept rattling, he walked down the hallway to check. "I approached his door, but…something told me not to open the door. I turned around and ran downstairs. I felt like something was behind me the whole time."

Noah left that home when he was eight, and eventually, the family ended up in the Deerfield Village apartment complex on Kendallville's east side. Can an apartment complex be haunted? Why not?

He and two of his brothers shared a room there, although the oldest was old enough to not have the same bedtime. As a result, it was just two of the boys who noticed the clothes in their closet sometimes moved—on their own. Pounding noises could be heard, too.

But Noah's scariest experience there came when he saw his father—saw him, despite the fact that the room was pitch dark. "But I could still see him….He was the maddest I've ever seen, and I was thinking, 'What did I do?' Then I blinked and really focused, and I didn't see it anymore." Although he speculates he might have actually been looking at a spare blanket in the dark, that doesn't seem to be his kind of luck.

Ten years later, he and his now-wife were living at Deerfield Village, we assume against his better judgement. He would sometimes wake up screaming and gasping for air, but Noah speculates that could have just been sleep apnea. Again, not with his luck.

That's not the only place in Kendallville where he had strange experiences. "During summer breaks from school I'd be out of the house most nights…. To me, nothing compares to a warm summer night taking a stroll through Kendallville, all alone—until you realize how the town has sounds and souls."

White Lady

Noah even once encountered the white lady, that famous ghost known across the country. "One morning before school started, I saw a lady in white while walking down Rush Street. It was overcast and, I believe, starting to rain, almost like a Hollywood moment." When he ran up the street to get another look at her, she was gone.

Noah thought he'd imagined her until he started hearing stories from others who saw her, too. The next summer, he was walking at the Elks Golf Course on the west side of town when a friend, a confirmed skeptic, glimpsed the woman in white from the corner of his eye before she again vanished. Noah said he never told his friend about his own sighting, but they both had enough sense to leave the area—quickly.

Kendallville's Elks naturally had an Antler's Club, designed for younger people and built in 1937. *Mike Mapes collection.*

The Benevolent and Protective Order of Elks, a nationwide organization, boasts in Kendallville a lodge, a large golf course and, in the '30s, an Antlers Club dedicated to younger members on the west side of the city. In addition to providing space for a round of golf, its course makes for good sledding in the winter and quiet walks at night, assuming the walks aren't interrupted by the supernatural.

Not far from that golf course is Sunset Park, a beautiful place for connecting with nature, picnics, ball games or an encounter with the supernatural. Noah was again walking with a friend when he had to stop for another kind of nature calling, and he made his way to the concession stand bathroom. His friend waited for him on Weston Avenue, a short distance away.

When Noah heard a man laughing, he assumed his friend had followed him all the way down there. "I called out for him, but I didn't hear a response." That was because when he left the bathroom, he found his friend still waiting on the other side of a street that runs along the park. No one else was around at that hour. It's safe to say Noah would have had something scared out of him if he hadn't already taken care of that business.

We stopped to look at the facility, and there's no way his friend could have sneaked up to it to scare him and then made it back across the street without being caught. We elected not to actually go into the building ourselves.

There were also reports of a haunting at a Main Street business called The Hairport, a beauty shop that's no longer in business. To our knowledge, Noah did not get his hair cut there.

So, haunted city or haunted person? We suspect Noah Shepherd would prefer it be the former.

17
Little Izzy

The house we lived in was insanely haunted.

The story Lilian Elizabeth Collins told is the most chilling one we encountered while researching this book. It took place along South Street in Kendallville, but don't bother looking, as the street name has been changed—unrelated to the haunting, we assume.

Don't bother looking up the age of the house, either. Official records list it as being built in 1900, but that's only because a fire destroyed many early records in Noble County. (The home the authors have lived in for many years is also listed as being built in 1900, but it actually dates to at least 1879.) The first Kendallville settler pitched his tent in 1833, and Kendallville was incorporated thirty years later, so when the house actually went up is anyone's guess. However, it seems to have been around long enough for three ghost stories to spring up around it—or maybe just two, but we'll explore that later.

We can only say that the house with the thing in the basement is old by Indiana standards.

The ghost that lives there is evil by *anyone's* standards. Well, one of the ghosts is…and maybe more. We'll get back to the basement later, too.

Lilian lived in the house for about twenty-five years. Although others had experiences there, hers might be a special case. "I'm in tune with those things. My friends would notice things but not like I would."

It was a gift her grandmother Rose Collins also had. "We'll have dreams and things will happen. I had a dream a month prior to [when] my husband's dad was in a car accident. I told my husband something's going to happen…

please tell him to be careful, I don't know what it is. A month later, he was in a really bad accident, totaled his truck out. I don't know—I just have very vivid dreams. My grandmother's the same way, [she] knew I was pregnant with both girls before I knew. I love being able to interact with the afterlife."

Some interactions with the afterlife go better than others. Take Little Izzy, for example.

Before we get to the bad stuff, let's talk about Izzy. How—or if—Izzy connects to the other ghosts in the house, we don't know, but she doesn't seem to be directly related to the family that generated the others. Was "Izzy" short for Elizabeth? There was a Mary Elizabeth Gerst, who was born the same year one of the other suspected ghosts died, but she lived to be seventy-one.

One explanation is that Izzy died in the home before the Gerst family lived there—so long ago that her story is sadly forgotten. But as we shall see, that's not the only explanation.

INVISIBLE FRIEND

Clues about Izzy came from Lilian's younger sister, Dazee, who was about six when she began making up—or repeating—strange stories. "They weren't like 'a bear broke into my house and ate my chocolate,'" Lilian said. "[She] actually went to school and told some of these crazy stories, and Mom and Dad had to go down to the police station—it was a complete mess." One of the stories was that her sister was babysitting her nephew when he drowned.

"Mind you, [she] didn't have a nephew." Lilian would know that, being the only older sister and about twelve years old at the time.

After their parents told the girl she could get into big trouble if she continued, "the lies would kind of stop when we were out in public, but they were really heavy still at home."

Meanwhile, the little girl became attached, as kids often do, to an invisible best friend. "One time we were…coming home from Auburn, and Dazee would not stop talking." After trying to get her to quiet down, their frustrated father stopped the car, opened the door and told the invisible friend to get out. "[She] had a complete meltdown…a legit mental break down at six or seven years old. Dad had to turn the car around to where they dropped off the friend, open the door and invite her friend back in."

Why was this happening? The question was answered when the first team of paranormal investigators came to the house. "It was very much not an invisible best friend," Lilian told us. "It was very much a ghost."

Accidents were common on early railroads. Many tales of hauntings involved crossings and bridges like this one, which once crossed the CSX Railroad near Albion. *Mark Hunter.*

Perhaps to keep her living friend from getting into any more trouble, Izzy came forward to the investigators. "She was having [Dazee] tell these stories so we would catch on that she was there."

Mission accomplished.

Once she'd been contacted, little Izzy explained she'd been hit by a train while walking to the store with her grandmother. Izzy may have been attached spiritually to something Lilian's parents later brought into the home, possibly a knickknack or used furniture. Or maybe Izzy just drifted there; the home is two blocks from the town's east–west railroad tracks. It's possible this kind of spirit transfer happens all the time, but less sensitive people never notice.

We were unable to find any news reports of a little girl dying that way in Kendallville, but such news items don't always survive a century or more of history. At the time, two railroad tracks crossed through Kendallville, so train-related mishaps were not unheard of.

SPOOKY DOLL

The little ghost also told the investigators she missed having a dolly, and that got the attention of Lilian's father, Gary Collins. "Dad really likes paranormal stuff.…He's not necessarily scared of it. So, Dad sent Mom out to buy a frickin' doll!"

The doll had tightly curled bangs, Lilian remembered, a detail that will become notable later. "So, they buy a doll, we wrap it up in a blanket, we lay it on the floor. Dad says, 'Izzy, this is your doll; no one else will play with it.' Dad had an EMF (electromagnetic field) detector, and it was going off like crazy."

One has to wonder what would have happened if Izzy didn't like the doll. A childhood temper tantrum would have to be especially scary coming from a preteen spirit. But that didn't turn out to be a problem.

"In the morning, the bangs on the doll had been moved. The whole doll smelled like must…and the bangs were smooshed to one side of its head, like she had snuggled with it all night long.

"Where that doll ended up after we moved we have no idea, but the poor thing was attached to it, and it probably wouldn't come out of that house."

Otherwise, Izzy made her age very clear, according to Lilian. "She loved the Christmas lights; she loved the Christmas tree." She also loved a karaoke machine with flashing lights. "We turned the lights on, and she would make the EMF reader go off like crazy." Between their experiences and the paranormal investigators, Lilian reported, "You could tell she was little. She hadn't started school yet, so she would have been six or younger when she passed."

Unlike some of the other spirits in the house, when Izzy made her presence known, it was in a more lighthearted way. Lilian said, "When they did the investigation, she came forward and said she liked to prank me all the time. My earbuds and stuff would come up missing."

One night, Lilian was sleeping downstairs (due to painting going on upstairs). "I was a heavy sleeper—until I had kids." But she still heard a woman yell, "Get up!" "I sat straight up in bed and said, 'What?' It was 2:00 a.m." Her parents, sleeping in an adjoining room, denied saying anything, let alone yelling.

On another occasion, Lilian's father fell asleep on the couch downstairs, his feet extending over the arm of the couch. "Ain't nothing waking him up [when he slept]," Lilian said. But somebody or something walked down the stairs and then yanked on Gary's big toe hard enough to wake him. He bounded to his feet, "ready to square up. That's one of those times when something scared him."

Since Izzy usually pranked Lilian and didn't try to scare anyone, Lilian speculated the spirit who scared her dad was not the little girl but Clayton Gerst.

Which brings us to a much darker part of the story.

18
The Thing in the Basement

Of course, not everything Lilian experienced was pleasant, especially when it came to the Gerst family.

Clayton Gerst was only nineteen when he had an altercation with his father in their shared home. It ended tragically. "He decided to take some poison and kill himself," Lilian said. "Family heard him moaning and groaning and found him at the top of the stairs. Doctors came, and they took him to the hospital, where he passed away."

He may have died at the hospital, "but he never left the house," said Lilian.

Let's back up a bit. Who is Clayton Gerst, and why did he die by suicide? What did he and his father argue about?

The father, Charles Edward Gerst, was born in 1875 and married Alice C. Carrick in 1896, which might very well be when they moved into the house. Charles worked at nearby Flint and Walling as a moulder, and according to his 1918 draft card, he was nearly blind in one eye. We don't know much about how he was as a father, but the couple had five children. Clayton James, who was born in 1897, died in 1916. That same year, Mary Elizabeth, the youngest Gerst, was born.

Since Charles is important to the story, we need to avoid confusion—or at least try to. So, to clarify, there were two Charles Gersts living in Kendallville: Charles Edward Gerst and Charles Edmond Gerst. They were born seven years apart and died within a year of each other. Edward—our guy—married Alice, while Edmond had a sister named Alice. There was also a third Alice Gerst (her father's name was Donald Robert), and untangling this gave us headaches. Fortunately for you, the reader, only one Alice Gerst figures into this story.

Which brings us back to Clayton.

News articles of the time confirm the "just the facts" part of the story. At age nineteen, Clayton Gerst got into an argument with his father, and at about 1:00 p.m., he drank four ounces of sulfuric acid in an attempt to end his life. We can only assume sulfuric acid was more commonly found in homes at the time. (It's still used around the home, especially in cleaning.) Neighbors tried to help by inducing vomiting to get the poison out, and then Drs. Williams and Goodwin arrived to continue treatment.

Clayton was taken to Lakeside Hospital, now the site of the Kendallville Public Library, for more treatment. At first, it was thought he might recover, but after several weeks, he suffered a relapse and passed away.

Why did he end his own life? The only fact we know for certain is that Clayton left a note behind, but the contents have never been revealed.

There were rumors, of course.

"Clayton didn't sound like he was the best person, from what I've heard," Lilian said. "And the way he's acting in the afterlife…I think Clayton knows he's not going to get the good end of the deal when it comes to heaven or hell."

Lilian spoke to some of Clayton's descendants, who told her the young man was going to school to be a priest—until he got an underage girl pregnant. Whether that started the fight, we don't know, but Clayton must have thought death by suicide was the only way out.

This is not confirmed, of course. Still, we had an opportunity to see photos of the young man and agree with Lilian's thoughts about him: "He looked like he was very mischievous, but he also looked like he could be a lady's man."

Mischievous ghosts, as any paranormal investigator will tell you, are the worst.

But Clayton Gerst's ghost is more than just mischievous. "He is the worst, and the scariest, and the most—I don't know what the word I'm looking for is," Lilian said. "He's the one who gave everyone the heebie-jeebies, the bad vibes—horrible."

But is Clayton also the thing in the basement?

Rotating Bedrooms

Things started to really peak when my sister and I went through our puberty phase.

This is not unheard of, as reported supernatural activity often increases with adolescents in the house. It also seemed worse when Lilian and her sister slept in the master bedroom, at the back of the home's second floor.

Their parents had the front bedroom. Often, there would be a game of musical beds of sorts, but "mainly I got stuck in that stupid master bedroom. I hated sleeping in that back bedroom. Nobody could sleep well there."

When Lilian had friends over, "Mom and Dad typically camped out in the living room, because we stayed up late and were loud." One friend was a witness to a terrifying moment in the master bedroom.

"We were spending the night, and we slept in Mom and Dad's bed. You know how when the TV goes black, you can see the reflection of everything behind you? At least in older TVs. I woke up in the middle of the night and saw someone standing in the doorway that divided the rooms. I just laid that for a minute, because I really thought someone had broken in and was waiting for us to wake up."

It wasn't her father: "Why would my Dad stand creepily in the door? I nudged my friend. 'Sierra, there's somebody standing in the doorway. Look at the TV.' So, she looks—she sees it, too." Like any reasonable people would, the two girls freaked out and ran for the stairs, but there was nothing in the doorway. Gary Collins searched the whole house, something that would become a routine, and found no evidence of a prowler.

Remember, it was upstairs where Clayton tried to end his life, and it's certainly possible his bedroom was up there, too.

"[My sister and] I went through a really hard depression phase when we were probably fourteen, fifteen, and stayed in that room. It's almost as if he would attach himself, because we would get so gloomy and depressed."

Haunted Cutout

At that time, Lilian's grandmother worked in a liquor store in downtown Kendallville. (Alcohol is not otherwise complicit in this story.) When an R&B singer named Ne-Yo started doing commercials for Malibu rum, the store got a life-size cardboard cutout of Ne-Yo.

"I wanted it, so my grandma got it for me," Lilian says. There were two closets in the master bedroom, a him-and-her combo. One had always, in Lilian's memory, been the woman's closet. "It was my closet, it was my mom's closet, the people before us....It's kind of weird how all women were in that closet. I put the cardboard cutout in front of that closet."

But the closet had problems. "It could be eight thousand degrees, we could have a heater in that closet, and it would grow mold. Mom and Dad did everything—Mom would bleach it."

After placing her decoration, Lilian had a feeling, as if she was being watched. "Stalked, almost, like...prey."

Her father blamed the cardboard Ne-Yo's eyes for freaking her out—at first.

"Finally, when things started happening to Dad...he started looking into it more. We had the first investigation team come in."

Enough time has passed that Lilian doesn't remember the name of one of the investigative teams, although she believes it was something like Ghost Hunters of Fort Wayne. The other, she says, is no longer in operation. These kinds of groups come and go, as members get busy in other areas of their lives.

In any case, the first investigation team, which came in when Lilian was a teen, had members who said they talked to Clayton Gerst himself. Clayton, they said, admitted he would stay in the women's closet and hide behind the cardboard cutout. This would explain why that closet was always cold and musty, despite everyone's best efforts. "They said he would hide behind that cutout and watch me. So, I absolutely destroyed that cutout—I cut it up, ripped it up, threw it away. Because, no, if you're going to watch me, you show yourself; that way, I can call you out."

This, by the way, is in no way a criticism of Ne-Yo or of Malibu.

The main goal of the first investigation team was to get rid of Clayton, and they apparently thought they had done this. Unfortunately, Clayton was too crafty for them.

"He didn't leave. He hides long enough for them to think he's gone...but he never leaves."

What about Charles?

"Charles, Clayton's father, died in the front downstairs bedroom," Lilian said. Charles Edward Gerst passed away at the age of seventy-seven in 1952 and was buried in Kendallville's Lake View Cemetery. His son was buried in Saint Mary's Catholic Cemetery in Avilla, but it appears neither of them stayed.

Located near Charles Gerst's workplace, Flint and Walling, traffic at Kendallville's Union Station gives a snapshot of Kendallville life at the time. *Noble County Historical Society*.

In a photo that was apparently taken at his workplace, Charles appeared to be a strong working man, typical of the tough people of the time. He really appears to be the type of person who would try to keep his children under control, even in the afterlife, and Lilian thinks that's exactly what he tries to do.

"He feels like it's his fault Clayton is still there and that Clayton is the way he is—like he feels bad they had that altercation and Clayton is stuck there." That was also the conclusion of one of two paranormal investigation teams that went through the house.

Lilian knows this not just because of investigation teams but also because she's seen Charles.

"I saw him in our doorway multiple times, almost like [he was] watching over us. I didn't feel scared or anything like that—watching over us, that's the vibes I felt. He was trying to protect us."

The investigators agreed. "[Charles] tried to keep Clayton in check so he'll leave me alone, because Clayton liked to screw with me. I would wake up, and I'd have bruises up and down my leg—unexplained bruises. I'm clumsy but not that clumsy. My sister would be the same way. She had bruises all over her. My sister would hear him [Clayton] whisper her name—she thought she was going crazy for a while."

It wasn't just the kids Clayton messed with. Lilian remembered one night, when the family had gone to bed but was still having a discussion between the rooms, *The Waltons* style. They were talking, coincidentally or not, about religion. "And when I'm talking about this, we heard the loudest *boom* downstairs. Dad thought for sure someone had busted a window and was breaking into the house."

At least that explanation would have made sense. Instead, the problem was with a chandelier that had been installed in the foyer a year or two earlier. "That chandelier had fallen completely out of the ceiling and shattered everywhere. There was no reason for it—it's almost as if someone completely untightened a screw." Nothing was broken or tampered with on the actual ceiling itself. "I'll never forget that."

Charles Gerst didn't have much luck when it came to curbing his son, but in fairness to him, Clayton seemed to be a spirit with a particularly large amount of dark energy. Was Charles's wife there, too?

Alice, Clayton's mother, passed away in the living room, also of old age. (She died in 1945.) Lilian said, "Her spirit, if it is there…we never noticed it. Obviously, with just lights flickering and things, we don't know who it is."

So, Clayton Gerst would seem to be the evil that inhabits this house, except for one little problem—but we'll get to that. It may seem like we're trying to build suspense, probably because we are.

Lilian, as one might expect, moved away as an adult. But when her parents separated, she and her husband were given a chance to take over the home payments and have the house as their own. "We would have said no, but the financial incentive was considerable."

Not long after moving back in, Lilian was dressing when she heard her husband sneaking upstairs to scare her. "I would scare him; I thought for sure he was trying to scare me. My mom was notorious; she used to pop up and scare me half to death." Feeling she was being watched, Lilian texted her mother, who was still living with them. But her mother confirmed Lilian's husband was outside.

"I looked up and saw…a shadow going up the stairs. I grabbed my clothes and went downstairs to finish getting ready."

Clayton—or something—had clearly not left.

DARK ENERGY

The thing in the basement. It's honestly…one of the scariest things I've encountered in my life. I've seen, heard, been touched. People can call me crazy—that's fine. I don't claim to be a medium.

But Lilian did speak to a medium, who agreed Lilian would notice these things more. "Because I was more in tune with it, and my dad was and my grandma was."

The medium's stark message: "There was something in the basement and it was dark. I knew it was dark—I hated going down to that basement. I would not go alone; I would not go without a light. I had to have a big flashlight with me when I had to go down there—hated it, hated it."

Clayton, right? Well, maybe.

The basement had a dark energy from the beginning. "I swear they had a portal in the basement and would just have their meetings down there." Lilian was the audience because of an air duct that led down there. "You could hear them talk and whisper and communicate."

What were they communicating about?

"I don't care," Lilian said.

It was the vent that finally convinced her father something was going on. Gary Collins was alone in the house, doing stretches on the living room floor, when he finally heard the whispers Lilian had been telling him about.

But that was far from the only evidence that some evil force remained in the home.

"Something would wake me up every single night, at 3:14 a.m. on the dot. I didn't know what it was. I didn't know what it wanted. I couldn't tell." (It should be noted that we don't know what time Clayton passed, other than "Thursday night.") "Well, I voiced to it, I said, 'Whatever it is, whoever it is, you need to come forward and let me know what you want, or you need to leave me alone.'"

After that, everything was fine—for one night.

"The next day, I dreamed of the scariest man I have ever seen in my life. It was an older man; his skin was gray; his eyes were evil, dark, dark circles around his eyes. He was in one of those flannel jackets, like the ones the old farmers wore. It was black and red and gray." Just as a reminder, no one in that house was a farmer. "He didn't say anything, he just stood there—and then ran at me, and I woke up in a panic."

It was a terrifying ordeal, which left Lilian certain of one thing: what she saw that night was the thing in the basement. "I could just tell."

Just one evil entity occupied the house, as far as anyone knows: Clayton Gerst. That left two questions. First, if Clayton died on the second floor, why haunt the basement? Second, why didn't it look like Clayton?

"I've seen pictures of Clayton, Charles....I have pictures of everyone in that family." We saw those pictures, too, and while Clayton did look like he could be a troublemaker, he didn't look like raw, pure evil. In fact, the thing in the basement didn't look like anyone in the family.

What Lilian saw that night did not resemble a Gerst.

An unknown number of years passed between when the house was built and when the Gersts occupied it, and there's no record of what happened during that interval. Did an earlier resident die there? Did someone get killed during construction? Was it built over an unmarked Native burial ground? Granted, early Natives wouldn't have been dressed like that. Or did Clayton become so twisted in his hatred and anger that he no longer looked himself?

Shadow Ghost

In any case, there were no more issues in the house—no more major issues, is how Lilian put it—until they suffered a water line break that filled the basement with a few feet of water.

"We had to tow Dad's stuff out that he left when he moved." Because Lilian was eight months pregnant, she stood in the basement, handing items to her husband, who did the hard work of carrying them up the stairs.

"I watched a dark figure....It shot from one side of the basement that was lighted, over to the dark, eerie-feeling side of the basement, and it literally took my breath away. I almost had a panic attack because I couldn't breathe—it felt like it was sitting on my chest."

Lilian and her husband traded places after that, although he didn't really want to go down there either after she told him what she saw. He had to do it for the rest of the stuff, but Lilian? "I don't care if a tornado comes here and blows me away; I'm not going down into that basement."

Although she never ventured down there again, it wasn't the end of the frights emanating from the basement. She would hear someone pounding on the basement door frequently. The bathroom and basement doors were set close together, and she once was trapped in the bathroom when she heard the basement door open and close and then someone banging outside. She called her mother, who arrived to find no one in the home—no one human. "I wasn't going to call 911 because I wasn't going to sound crazy—I knew it was something nobody else could see. I got the heebie-jeebies just talking about him."

Lilian's determination for the rest of her time in the home remained: "I don't care if there's a twister coming—I'm going to hang onto that bathtub."

Eventually, the family sold the house, and despite her experiences, Lilian decided to do one more walkthrough. "That was twenty-four years of my life....I wanted to walk through it one last time to make sure I got everything and say goodbye." One last thing she wanted was a bedframe her father had built. But before her family arrived to help her move it, "I got a super eerie feeling, and I just needed to get out of the house. I shut the door behind me and locked it." She decided to wait on a folding chair near the entrance to the garage. That's where she was when she heard the door, which she had closed and locked, open. Then it slammed shut, hard. "If that window had been glass...it would have shattered."

It was the last time Lilian ever set foot in the house.

Her mother went in to retrieve the last few items, and while she was in the front room, someone loudly yelled in her ear, "Get out!" But of course, no one was there.

So, who—or what—is the thing in the basement? The number one suspect is still Clayton Gerts, of course. Perhaps the pull between wanting to become a priest and giving in to carnal desires tortured his soul beyond bearing.

Others have had experiences there, too, but the medium's opinion that Lilian was sensitive to the supernatural explains why hers were so much more vivid. Experienced paranormal investigators were convinced, and the backstory certainly tracks.

Maybe the thing in the basement is still there, waiting for the next supernaturally sensitive person to victimize.

19

SPIRITED LIGONIER

Ligonier is a historic Jewish community of about five thousand people named after a Pennsylvania town. (Ironically, both lie along the Lincoln Highway. To make the matter more confusing, the Ligonier in the other state isn't all that far from Indiana, Pennsylvania.) Thanks to its connection to Kidd and Company, Ligonier was once the marshmallow capital of the world. If you wish to add a joke about the Stay-Puft Marshmallow Man from *Ghostbusters*, we could hardly blame you.

As we saw earlier while covering the Ligonier Public Library, the community is also home to ghosts.

On a related note, the Ligonier Public Library owned, for a time, one of the few surviving eighteenth-century synagogues still standing in the United States. At one time, the city of Ligonier had one of the area's largest Jewish populations, and in 1889, the Ahavath Sholom Reform Temple was built to serve them.

Decades later, the building was donated to the library, and the Ligonier Historical Museum occupied it for three decades. But after an expansion project, the library could no longer afford to maintain the structure, and it was sold to become a private home.

We're not certain where all the museum items ended up, but if any of them happen to have a spirit anchored to it and ended up in the library, it's in good company.

A Martin Street resident reported they and their friends saw strange shadows in their home and once saw a little girl in white who seemed to be

Built in 1889, the Ahavath Sholom Reform Temple served a large Jewish community in the Ligonier area and later became the Ligonier Historical Museum. *Mark Hunter.*

trying to reach out toward them. A young woman was heard crying there another time.

On South Main Street, the claim is made that a friendly ghost haunts another home. She sometimes appears on the home's stairs in one of those "corner of your eye" sightings, and she's also been seen in a hallway mirror. According to the report, in the mirror, she can be seen going up and down the stairs. A little boy has appeared in the basement, and even a ghost cat is claimed to occupy the place. In addition, electrical items sometimes turn on and off, even when they're not plugged in, and a crying girl can be heard in the dining room.

That's a whole lot of hauntings for one place. Just the same, the occupant said they have always felt safe in the residence.

HAUNTED DESK

Nothing is quite so scary to a writer as the idea of a haunted desk—well, maybe nothing except a publishing deadline. At still another Ligonier home, an anonymous website poster said that when their mother was young, a man rented the upstairs area from the family. When the renter moved, he left a desk behind.

There had been no mystical experiences in the home before, and the witness played with the desk without giving it a thought. That's when things got strange.

The witness said she was climbing the stairs one day when she heard footsteps behind her and turned, only to see nothing but her parents sitting on the couch.

Another time, she had a friend over who went to the restroom and came back just a few minutes later to say that she'd heard her host's mother knocking on the door, telling her to hurry because the mother's stomach hurt. But the other girl had just watched her mother and father leave.

The witness had other experiences, including hearing knocking noises, but she refused to tell the poster all the experiences for fear of scaring them.

After that, the poster heard a disembodied voice speaking and saw a rocking chair move on its own. When they were going to sleep, something would tap them on their backs.

The poster's conclusion is that some kind of essence was attached to the desk, and that might explain why the mysterious renter left it behind.

Many investigations have focused on that very thing: objects that ghosts are somehow attached to. How this happens isn't certain, but it does give one pause when it's time to go antique shopping.

It should be noted, by the way, that the Ligonier in Pennsylvania also has its share of ghost stories.

20
The Old Jail Museum

This is a difficult subject for us to write about, because, well, there's nothing to write about. And there should be. (Stand by for a twist, though.)

The Old Jail Museum, while it looks like it has to be haunted, has never had a report of ghost sightings that we're aware of. This puts it in the "should be but isn't" category, because let's face it, the place looks like it has to have some ghosts in it.

Just the same, and despite the fact that some inmates have surely died while in custody, there don't seem to be any spirits inside. That's great, because it is, after all, a museum. People should be concentrating on the exhibits rather than the possibility of supernatural beings tapping them on the shoulder.

The Old Jail was built in 1875—at the time, it was called the New Jail—and listed in the National Register of Historic Places in 1982. Between those dates, in 1967, it was closed after a new jail was built on the east side of Albion. It's now the oldest public building in Noble County.

(Interestingly, another Noble County Jail was also turned into a museum in Noble County, Ohio.)

The building housed both the jail and a residence for the Noble County sheriff, with the sheriff's wife often cooking for the inmates and serving as matron for female offenders. So, there was a lot of life while the jail was in service…and only a little death.

A Noble County sheriff and his family pose in front of his residence and job, now the Old Jail Museum. *Noble County Historical Society*.

One inmate hanged himself in the building in 1918. On the other hand, two babies were born in the same structure to wives of the sheriffs. Maybe it all balances out. Maybe it doesn't. About twenty thousand inmates went through its doors, vastly outnumbering the three dozen Noble County sheriffs.

Probably the most infamous inmate of the jail was Marvin Kuhns, who developed, through sad experience, expertise in escaping the jail. Kuhns, a notorious horse thief who was apparently well liked by anyone whose horse he didn't steal, escaped from the Noble County Jail no less than three times. Once, he got away by stealing a horse from the jail's stable. The other two times, he stole horses *and* buggies.

DEATH OF A HORSE THIEF

Although he was buried in Wolf Lake Cemetery, Kuhns met his end in 1907 after he stole a horse and buggy near Van Wert, Ohio. Authorities there tracked him down, and he died in a gunfight.

It should be noted that Noble County's horse thieves reportedly had their den just west of Wolf Lake, where they were said to keep up to thirty head of stolen horses in a stable. Next to it stood a tavern they frequented until their leader, Gregory McDougle, was hanged in 1858, and the gang was broken up.

We're not suggesting Kuhns and McDougle are connected—aside from them both being horse thieves. McDougle died forty-nine years before Kuhns did, so it can be assumed they didn't share the same tavern stools. So, if Kuhns stayed around as a spirit, where would he be? It's doubtful he'd show up at the Noble County Jail, a place he constantly sought to escape.

It's also unlikely that he showed up to reunite with Delia Bird, his fifteen-year-old sweetheart, who stayed with him at his father's Green Township home for several weeks. They took a trip to Fostoria, Ohio, in 1890, where Kuhns showed his true colors. He robbed her of not only cash but also her bracelets, just before he was captured by the police—again. Somehow, Kuhns got the idea that she had ratted him out to the Fostoria Police, and who could blame her?

Dalia insisted she didn't rat him out, but she did want him hanged on general principles. Again, who could blame her?

Perhaps he still haunts the Wolf Lake area, where he was born and died, or the area where his parents made their Green Township home. Maybe he even haunts the Stanley Schoolhouse at Chain o' Lakes State Park. The original schoolhouse there was, according to some, burned down by Kuhns.

Or it could be that he stayed close to his wife Catherine Hagan, whom he married in 1905. That was after he robbed and abandoned Delia Bird, so let's not judge. To complicate matters, he had a wife before Delia: Kate Mourie. Or perhaps Catherine Hagan and Kate Mourie were the same people, as one source suggests, although that makes the timeline wrong. Maybe Kate haunted *him*.

Kuhns was, by all accounts, a charming man, and he charmed his way into a pardon by the governor of Ohio the same year he married Catherine. She had been his greatest advocate, along with many others,

The Wolf Lake Cemetery grave of Noble County's most notorious outlaw, Marvin Kuhns, who met his death in a gun battle. *Emily Hunter.*

including Fort Wayne Police Officer Joseph Kennelly, who encountered Kuhns in a Churubusco shootout—and was shot by him.

Kennelly wrote, "While I was severely wounded, I have never had anything but the most kindly feeling toward Mr. Kuhns....I assure you that nothing would afford me greater pleasure than to see Marvin Kuhns a free man."

You can't buy that kind of charm.

In any case, Kuhns died of his own gunshot wounds just two years after marrying Catherine, who lived to be seventy-five. Although Catherine never mentioned it and may not have known, it would hardly be surprising if Marvin accompanied her in his afterlife.

Some clichés are real, such as the sheriff's wife cooking for the inmates or trusty bloodhounds on the standby in case of an escape. Still, contrary to what you might have seen on old TV shows with the name Andy Griffith in

It wouldn't be a small-town sheriff's department without bloodhounds, always prepared to sniff out the bad guys. *Noble County Historical Society*.

the title, rural sheriffs often faced violence in the line of duty. During one of his escapes, Kuhns knocked Sheriff George McLean senseless. John Cleland was stabbed while in office between 1910 and 1914. Sheriff Irvin Cazier was wounded and a LaGrange County deputy was killed in the manhunt for a suspect who robbed the Kendallville A&P store and shot a clerk.

Maybe the Old Jail Museum isn't haunted because none of the former inmates had any interest in reliving—if it could be called that—their experiences there.

That said, there are articles inside the museum that would, if this were an episode of *Supernatural*, be holding on to some spirits. Weapons, for instance—there's a cannon in there, for crying out loud, not to mention military uniforms and weapons from several wars—which often carry spirits. There's also a note carved into a piece of stone by what may have been the first white man to visit Noble County. He came here, not voluntarily, but as a guest of the Natives.

The lack of haunting figures will be a disappointment to ghost hunters, of course. Just the same, the Old Jail and its pieces of history are fascinating to tour, and it's open on Saturday afternoons through summer.

The Real Haunted Jail

And now, the twist:

The *new* Noble County Jail is haunted.

The present Noble County Jail, on the east end of Albion, was completed in 1999. It's actually the fourth to be built in Albion. The first was the log cabin on the west side of the courthouse square; the second, around the corner, is now the Old Jail Museum; and the third went up in 1967, and part of it was incorporated into the present sheriff's department/jail. There have been deaths on the newer property before, both before and after the present building was finished, but no ghost story can be pinned to a specific spirit.

The building is solid and, although it's a quarter of a century old as of this writing, technologically advanced.

And it has a ghost in its proverbial machine.

Witnesses report electronic doors locking and unlocking by themselves and toilets suddenly flushing with no one around them. Sometimes, people just plain get spooked. A shadowy figure has been seen on catwalks between the cellblocks. The jail officers call it "Steve."

21
HANG 'EM HIGH

The office of sheriff is a powerful and important elected position in Indiana these days, but it wasn't always quite so highly regarded. John Humphries was elected Noble County sheriff in 1836, but he found the job just wasn't worth his time. Instead, he traded the office for a shotgun from Mason Merriam, whom he defeated in the election.

Yes, one side traded their office for a shotgun. It was a different time.

They each probably thought they got the better part of the trade, but Humphries must have breathed a sigh of relief when he discovered he'd missed out on the chance to hang someone.

It was the only legal hanging ever conducted in Noble County—but it was not the only hanging. We'll come back to that.

The Noble County seat, at the time, was located in Augusta, about two miles west of where Albion would one day be. The courthouse in Augusta burned down in March 1843—with some criminal help—so a lot of the official paperwork was destroyed. Still, the story comes down to us from former Noble County Sheriff Nathaniel Eagles and Washington Coon, whose parents operated the tavern in Augusta (taverns being one of the first businesses that sprang up in new communities).

Speaking of alcohol, the whole affair started in the village of Rochester, east of Ligonier, in 1840. Four men were target shooting, their aims affected one way or another by the cheap whiskey they were drinking.

Soon, John Farley and John Lechner began arguing over a twenty-five-cent bet, again fueled by alcohol. The story goes that Farley threw Lechner

The first Noble County Courthouse, in Augusta, was the scene of the only legal death penalty verdict in county history. *Noble County Historical Society*.

to the ground, and Lechner came up with a gun and pulled the trigger but missed the other man. Farley ran to a board fence and, from its top, began verbally and profanely abusing Lechner. After all, Lechner's gun was empty.

That's when Lechner grabbed another man's loaded gun, took aim and shot Farley in the chest.

The trial was presided over by Judge James Wright, who later told the story to Eagles and Coon. There wasn't much story left to tell, as the jury was made up of "eye for an eye" types. Lechner was held in the Augusta Hotel—there being no jail at the time—and three weeks later, he was taken to a location about half a mile west of town, where many area residents gathered. There, in a location now unknown, Lechner was hanged.

It happened east of town, according to one old-timer Helen Kimble, whose grandfather Joseph Beal came to Noble County in 1834, and who said her mother showed her the tree when she was nine years old. It probably made quite the anti-crime impression on her. Helen said a platform, complete with a trapdoor, had been built under the tree and that around 1,500 people from at least four states came to witness the execution.

Lechner's end was even more ignoble afterward. His body was taken to his sister's residence, a home built by Levi Perry, one of Noble County's first settlers. Covered in corn fodder in a barn, it remained there, frozen, for several weeks, before it was moved to a nearby woods.

Finally, he was buried in Perry Township, but the location has since been forgotten.

So, if you live in the general Ligonier area, your house might be built over John Lechner's bones. Don't let your imagination take over.

Horse Thieves and Diamond Hill

The same year as Lechner's legal hanging came another hanging that was very much *not* legal. That technicality didn't stop the Noble County Regulators from pursuing their own form of justice, and it left a haunted hill in its wake.

In the early 1800s, Noble County was part of the Wild West, and things got wild, indeed. In fact, Northeast Indiana became known across the country and beyond for its lawlessness. Outlaws took to the many swamps to hide, communication was poor and someone could commit a crime in one town with the people of the next town being none the wiser. According to Weston Goodspeed, in his *History of Noble County*, the area was "notorious for being the citadel of all villains."

Those villains tended to congregate in an area called the Tamarack Swamp, near the town of Rome, now Rome City. Every kind of criminal abounded, but our interest lies in one of the most heinous crimes of the era: horse thieving.

When the State of Indiana passed a law in 1852 allowing the formation of local crime fighting organizations, groups of "regulators" formed. The regulators began rounding up suspected criminals, and we imagine the words those bad guys feared the most were "get a rope." One of the suspects narrowly escaped hanging after the men in Ligonier voted on whether to apply a noose and decided against it by one vote.

Not all were so lucky. The roundup also netted Gregory McDougle, and when the regulators brought him in, a U.S. deputy marshal told them McDougle was accused of robbery, jail break and murder in Canada.

Canada? At a time when people rarely traveled? Well, it's possible. One of the other criminal leaders was Silas Doty (often called Sile), who lived in Steuben County but was, in his time, one of the best-known criminals in the United States. He actually wrote an autobiography! It's certainly possible McDougle, like Doty, could have ended up in Canada while fleeing authorities. Besides that, according to some accounts, McDougle was from Canada to begin with.

The regulators this time voted for the alleged horse thief to stretch a rope.

So, in January 1858, McDougle was hanged from a large oak tree at Diamond Lake Hill (also called Diamond Hill), which overlooks Diamond Lake southeast of Ligonier. In a letter to the *Noble County American*, Helen Kimble said the hanging happened "very close to where the Ligonier people have their pleasure resort." Since we haven't found any information about that resort, her statement wasn't all that helpful.

There's a conflicting story of a cottonwood tree locals call the "hanging tree." That, they say, is where all the horse thieves were hanged—from what's said to be the largest cottonwood in Indiana.

The problem is that the tree isn't located on Diamond Hill—it's actually just across a road from Diamond Lake, at the base of the hill but at lake level. There's also, of course, the fact that McDougle is the only alleged horse thief hanged there—at least that anyone will admit to. Just the same, although news reports say the guilty tree was an oak, they don't say McDougle was hanged *on* the hill but *at* the hill.

As for this being the largest cottonwood in Noble County, we weren't able to corroborate that. However, we have seen the tree. We didn't take a picture, as it stands on private property, along a stretch of road with curves that make it dangerous to stop. (Also, because one of us, Mark, is not supposed to be near cottonwoods if he happens to be breathing at the time.)

Just the same, we can confirm it's one *big* tree.

McDougle confessed to stealing thirty-four horses in the previous year, as well as robbing stores, tanneries and peddlers. He also admitted to counterfeiting, a common problem in those days, and breaking out of jail twice. He insisted, however, that he wasn't guilty of murder.

Just the same, regulators from Noble, LaGrange, Steuben and DeKalb Counties showed up to watch the hanging—and to send a message.

McDougle was buried in a cemetery just north of Rome City, and at one point, a portrait of the regulators who hanged him, well, hung in the DeKalb County Courthouse.

Communication towers top Diamond Lake Hill and overlook Diamond Lake. One of the towers might be in the footprint of a now-gone haunted house. *Mark Hunter.*

It was the beginning of the end for the gangs of criminals controlling Noble County, but it was just the beginning of McDougle's story.

You see, Gregory McDougle stuck around.

Maybe the view was good. At 1,050 feet, Diamond Hill is reportedly the fifth highest of Indiana's named summits. (We've hiked to the second highest, Hell's Point in Steuben County, which is aptly named.) Or maybe McDougle is hanging around, pardon the phrase, looking for the wife and young child he left behind or for justice—or both.

Ghost Laying

We wonder if some locals might have forgotten about the hanging's location by the time seventy years passed. That's when local farmers launched a ghost hunting expedition to that very same hill.

The problem was apparently long in coming and made such a ruckus that it was reported on by the *Garrett Clipper*, a newspaper in the next county over, in an issue that was printed on Halloween 1927. At that time, a deserted farm stood on the hill, with a barn and a deteriorating house described by the *Clipper*: "The roof is caving in and window casements falling out. There the ghost is said to make his dwelling." It had apparently been an impressive place in the day, with the house made of black walnut and the barn "fashioned by a master artisan of pioneer days." Now, the home and surrounding fields were choked by weeds, and "an atmosphere of death hangs over the vicinity."

Residents in the area of Wawaka, a short distance away, described strange lights, moans and even sightings of the ghost. Nothing happened there during the day, but at night, the property became so active that people—at least those within earshot—got tired of it.

"They are planning an old-fashioned ghost laying party," the *Clipper* reported.

From what we can gather, that means laying the ghost to rest, although the locals seemed to be thinking more of lying in wait for whoever might be impersonating a ghost. Convinced the haunting was being carried out by someone who was more flesh and blood, a group of farmers and their wives determined to spend the night in the house. Strength in numbers, perhaps.

"The scoffers only smile," the *Clipper* concludes, "and promise to bring back something more tangible than a ghost when they pay their call."

The story attracted such attention that it was sent out by the United Press and ended up in, among other places, the *Indianapolis Times*.

So…what did they find?

That's another haunting mystery. We've been unable to locate any report about what transpired that night. Maybe it means the locals found nothing and slinked home in embarrassment about all the fuss. Maybe they saw something that scared them so badly, they were afraid to ever speak of it. Maybe the whole group disappeared, never to be seen again. OK, that last bit is unlikely, since their vanishing would be news in itself.

There was follow-up news, of a sort, published in the *Hammond Lake County Times* on December 11, 1928 (and presumably other newspapers, as with the first story). Margaret Ott found the article and pointed it out to us.

Whatever happened over a year before, the attempt by local residents to quiet the ghost—or flesh and blood people imitating ghosts—seemed to work. According to Mr. and Mrs. C.H. Trestler, who had a home on the side of the hill, there had been no signs of occupation or other problems in the abandoned house for some time—at least not until they noticed two automobiles drive up the hill to the former farm. Not long after, the witnesses said, they heard the screams of two men and saw lights in the unoccupied home.

Again, we were unable to uncover any follow-up to the article, although we continue the search when the opportunity presents itself. Were the vehicles seen leaving? Or did they eventually get towed away when the drivers never appeared to claim them? We were also unable to find the Trestler property on old Noble County Plat Books.

It may be that we simply haven't yet stumbled on updates to either story and they remain hidden away in newspaper archives.

In any case, if you hear or see any strange happenings on Diamond Lake or the hill nearby, it might just be McDougle, swinging in the breeze. He and Lechner, who died about two miles from each other, are the only recorded non-suicide hangings in Noble County history.

There were, sadly, many suicides by hanging in Albion's history. One was recorded in 1872 by the *New Albany* (IN) *Ledger Standard*. A well-to-do farmer, said to be upset by domestic troubles, threw a rope over the limb of a tree to carry out the act. A note of interest is that it happened about half a mile northwest of Wawaka, putting it only a mile or so from Diamond Lake.

22

CANALS, DAMS AND CHAIN O' LAKES

For a time during the early history of the United States, canals were all the rage. Roads tended to be questionable, at best, and wagons plodded along, requiring horses or other animals. Railroads hadn't arrived, so water remained a preferred way to travel.

Northern Indiana, then part of the Northwest Territory, was a maze of rivers and swamps. It often looked more like one big lake, especially in the spring. In fact, the westernmost *naval* battle of the American Revolution happened in Indiana—but that's a story for another time.

The first completed canal in America, along the Connecticut River, was signed on for by Massachusetts Governor John Hancock—yes, that John Hancock. It led to a spate of canal building, and a young Indiana joined in. Only twenty years old, the Indiana government took out loans to fund the Mammoth Improvement Act.

This brings us back to Noble County. The canal system, planned to connect the Ohio River with Lake Erie, would need feeder lakes to keep the water level up. Dams can be a double-edged sword, of course. They brought hydraulic power for industries but also tended to collapse. Port Mitchell, a few miles south of Albion, was the county seat in 1884 and was a growing, vibrant community, thanks, in part, to a dam. But the dam collapsed, and Port Mitchell lost the county government to Albion. Now, it's just a small collection of homes.

This didn't stop the state government, which was determined to build a dam that would store water for dry spells at a place called Northport in

Orange Township. Reportedly, the construction foreman divided his workers up, housing French laborers in Northport and Irish workers on the other side of the dam project, where another town was developing.

The two groups didn't get along. So, when the French were assigned to work on the south side, the foreman warned them to "do as the Romans do," which explains how Rome City got its name.

The dam, officially named the Northport Dam, did get built. But it was never used to feed canals, as the Mammoth Improvement Act sent the state into bankruptcy after just four years. One part of the feeder canal that exists today runs along Canal Road, ironically used for automobile traffic.

Sylvan Lake itself was so successful that the town of Rome City grew around it, and it became a huge tourist draw. The famous author Gene Stratton Porter built a home along its shores, and it's now a boater's paradise.

But the price of that success came in human lives.

The dam broke three times and threatened to break twice more. The first time it broke, in 1839, came before the work was even finished. In 1855,

The 1974 super outbreak brought a tree down on author Gene Stratton Porter's historic home. *Noble County Historical Society.*

the dam gave way near its outlet, often called the Tumbles in later years. In 1877, a flood endangered it again, and only fast, hard work saved it.

Every time the dam collapsed, the rushing water did a great deal of damage downstream, sometimes for miles. But it was in 1844 that one of those disasters took three lives.

The workers on the dam were caught in the washout and lost, presumed drowned by the sudden flood. One was later found floating in a small pond downstream from the dam, possibly Spring Lake along Sycamore Park.

The other two bodies were never located. Considering the amount of water that washed downstream, it's hard to tell where they finally settled.

In 1882, an early chronicler of Noble County history, Weston Goodspeed, counted eleven other deaths on Sylvan Lake itself, but he also said, "This has often been owing to their own carelessness."

In addition to that, we're told Big Island, also called Boy Scout Island, toward the east side of the lake, is haunted. Supposedly, two people died on the island: one in the 1974 tornado outbreak and one from a fire. We confirmed a Sylvan Lake man was killed when his "island home" was hit by the twister, but we're told that occurred on a neighboring island, although there was severe tornado damage on Big Island. We also weren't able to find any details about a fire. Five people were killed in Noble County during the super outbreak, two of them a mother and child who were killed in a mobile home. The lake level had to be lowered the next year to allow the removal of debris.

There's also the August Willing Castle, an impressive-looking lakefront home that was rumored to belong at one point to actress Carole Lombard (whose family actually had a lake home a short distance away). Called a castle because of its single tower, it was said to be the final "unresting" place of a neighbor named Mrs. Phillips, who, according to the story, was killed by her husband with an axe before he set their home on fire.

Why would Mrs. Phillips's ghost then move into the nearby castle? Well, her home was gone, so perhaps she just liked the new digs. According to a post on the Castles of the United States website, a family with two daughters later moved in, and the girls told their schoolmates about seeing a ghost there. They reacted badly on learning the spirt could be that of the murdered woman or her husband.

We were unable to substantiate the murder story. But interestingly, in 1918, the Noble County Jail had an inmate named A.H. Phillips of Rome City, who, according to jail records, had been judged insane.

The Sylvan Lake spillway, often called The Tumbles, provided a play area for daring youths. *Noble County Historical Society.*

Damage from the 1974 super outbreak, which killed five people in Noble County and dumped debris into Sylvan Lake. *Grace Leatherman Collection.*

The early dead have been long forgotten, so the noises and whispers heard in the night downstream of Sylvan Lake, the strangely cool breezes, the feelings of something off, can't be blamed on one specific spirit. After all, nature seems to rule in that rural Noble County area, and nature provides a chorus of its own. That's probably all it is.

Probably.

CABIN FEVER

Chain o' Lakes State Park is a beautiful jewel in Noble County's crown. It's also haunted.

For many years after Natives were supplanted by white settlers, the area in Green Township had scattered farms, fields, swamps and, of course, a chain of lakes. The state park was established in 1960, and over time, the

Notorious local outlaw Marvin Kuhns allegedly burned down the first Stanley Schoolhouse, and its replacement is now a Chain o' Lakes State Park learning center. *Mark Hunter.*

fields became woods and meadows. It was a rocky start. Although the state park had wide support, there was also some opposition, and early on, many of the old homes and barns on the new park land were leveled by arsonists. There was the occasional drowning, as unfortunately happened in so many lakes over the years.

Whether any of that is related to later reports of the supernatural isn't certain. We can testify that the wooded trails can seem a little spooky after dark, but apparently, some areas are spookier than others.

Specifically, one of the park's rustic rental cabins is haunted, although, for the sake of preventing problems down the road, we won't say which one. Park security and housekeeping employees have reported odd happenings, such as doors suddenly flinging open or already open doors slamming shut.

Rumor is that the Chain o' Lakes Campground is also haunted, but we've spent a lot of time there and never noticed anything odd. Still, it should be noted that an old Native burial mound, scarred from an invasion by archaeologists many years ago, stands just a short distance from the campground.

A Native village also stood along the north side of Bowen Lake (then called Indian Lake), and it can be assumed Natives were buried near there. However, that location isn't close to either the cabins or the campground.

In our mind, the spookiest thing you're likely to encounter is the sound of coyotes at night or possibly angry squirrels battling each other—unless you pick that one haunted cabin. Have fun choosing.

23

Tragic Deaths, But No Hauntings

It was almost a theme in our research: the incidents and places we thought would most likely result in hauntings, such as the courthouse or the old jail, simply didn't. Or no one came forward to report them, of course. So, here are a few historical incidents around Noble County that should have produced some unsettled spirits.

In 1884, Martin Sellers of Kendallville was called to testify in a murder trial. He and the accused, Columbus C. Cain, must have been very good friends, because Sellers was heard to say he would kill himself rather than testify. Sure enough, Sellers went to his room a short time later and shot himself, a story that made headlines in newspapers from North Dakota to the *New York Times*.

It's not certain whether Sellers was staying at one of the Albion hotels during the trial or whether he killed himself in his home in Kendallville. So, who knows? Maybe a place that has had supernatural happenings is hosting Sellers's ghost. Albion's Worden House Hotel was divided into three parts and moved to become private residences, and one of those, on South Street, is reported to be haunted—maybe that's where Sellers was staying.

As for the accused, we can say with some certainty that, if he was found guilty, his conviction did not result in execution. We couldn't find any reports of the trial, but Columbus C. Cain was jailed on charges of public intoxication in 1891 and assault and battery in 1889. If it's the same person—and we think it was—he was free as little as five years after the trial.

An overhead view of Albion's courthouse square, likely dating from the 1950s. *Noble County Historical Society*.

In 1903, Columbus C. Cain was a resident of Orange Township, but he was at his son's residence in Kendallville when he got a piece of steak stuck in his throat and expired as his family tried to help him.

Black Pine Animal Sanctuary

Black Pine Animal Sanctuary takes in just about every type of abandoned or mistreated exotic animal with the aim of giving them a place to live in peace and comfort for the rest of their lives. Black Pine is now a few miles west of Albion in the Noble County 4H Park, but when it first began, it was located on the west edge of town, bordering Rose Hill Cemetery.

As a result, cemetery visitors could actually look over a fence and see camels and emus wandering a meadow. No one has reported a haunting at either Black Pine location—by either humans or animals—but that didn't mean it couldn't scare people.

One of its residents was Mufasa, a great lion who passed away several years ago. A lion's roar doesn't necessarily sound like what you hear in

Before he passed away, Mufasa lived at the Black Pine Animal Sanctuary, and his spine-tingling roar traveled for miles. *Mark Hunter.*

movies or TV, but it's certainly attention-grabbing, especially if you're not used to hearing it.

We heard it because there's a valley to the west of our house, and some audio trick allowed Mufasa's roar to come straight in our bedroom window, as if he was standing right outside. Hearing a lion roar in your ear while you're sleeping is an exciting experience, to put it mildly.

More Sylvan Lake

In addition to the dam collapses at Sylvan Lake, tragedies all around the area are remembered by numerous people. Drownings are common, at least when added up over time, but as every lake person knows, that goes for any lake that has human activity on it.

Locals report, among other things, a couple who died when they drove off a bridge into Sylvan Lake; a car driven out on the winter ice that fell through; a snowmobile that suffered the same fate; and at least two people who passed away when they were overrun by speed boats. One of those was particularly tragic, as it involved a young boy. There was also at least one death by suicide, when a woman jumped off the dam.

In 1890, a man named Frank Bollinger was skating across the lake and pushing before him a barrel of oil that proved too heavy for the ice. His drowning was reported by the *Indianapolis News* as occurring on "Rome City Lake."

In another incident, some kids were playing at a gravel pit just north of the dam when a landslide caught them by surprise, killing one of them. None of those deaths have been connected to a specific haunting.

A LIVING SKELETON

By all accounts, Mr. Mains, who lived in Albion in the early 1850s, was a normal man. However, physical ailments had him wasting away, and he was described as "skin and bone" by George Roof in his 1908 *Popular History of Noble County*. "He did not die," Roof added, "in the sense of dying, but lay down in an unrecognizable transition."

Flint and Walling windmills were once shipped around the world, and some have since found their way back. *Mike Mapes collection.*

The surprise came when Mr. Mains was exhumed in 1897, to be reburied in what became Rose Hill Cemetery. "There appeared to be no outward change from life, except the vital organs were not active." In other words, the man had not decayed. At all. Maybe some of the ghosts we see are people who just aren't completely certain they're dead.

We're also surprised there are no known hauntings at The Mid-America Windmill Museum, near Kendallville. That city's oldest manufacturer was reportedly Flint and Walling, which built windmills and shipped them around the world. Many of those windmills made their way back to the museum, and one can only wonder what kind of stories surrounded their use and eventual recovery. It's said that American soldiers encountered Flint and Walling windmills in Africa during World War II.

A Real Barn Burner

Finally, and ranging a bit far from our subject matter, we have the case of arsonist Henry Rosenberger. In 1896, he was sentenced to a five-year prison stint at Indiana Prison North after setting fire to several buildings on the Kendallville fairgrounds the year before. Tragically, the fire destroyed $16,000 in not only property but also horses.

A Kendallville hearse, ready to take the deceased to their final resting place in style. *Mike Mapes collection.*

We could imagine Rosenberger being haunted in his jail cell by flaming horses, which is the only nebulous connection we could make to the subject of ghosts.

But the most interesting part of the story for us is that a man who was making a speech at the fairgrounds when the fires broke out had to interrupt his presentation because of the excitement. The speaker? Claude Matthews, the governor of Indiana.

BIBLIOGRAPHY

"Albion, Indiana Ghost Sightings." Ghosts of America. https://www.ghostsofamerica.com/4/Indiana_Albion_ghost_sightings.html.

Alvord, S.E. *Alvord's History of Noble County, Indiana*. B.F. Bowen, 1902. https://archive.org/details/alvordshistoryof00alvo.

Bunting, C.R. "Noble County's Desperado." *Connections: The Hoosier Genealogist 53*, no. 1 (October 1, 2013,): 25. www.indianahistory.org.

Dingman, F.A. *Obituaries and News Items of Early Settlers of Noble County, Indiana.* Albion New Era, 1882.

Goodspeed, W.A. *Counties of La Grange and Noble, Indiana. Historical and Biographical.* F.A. Battey & Co., 1882.

———. *Counties of Whitley and Noble, Indiana*. F.A. Battey & Co., 1882. https://archive.org/details/alvordshistoryof00alvo.

"Haunted Churches in Indiana." Unexplainable.net. https://www.unexplainable.net/ghost-paranormal/haunted-churches-in-indiana-iii.php.

"Haunted Places in Indiana." The Shadow Lands. http://www.theshadowlands.net/places/indiana.htm.

"Haunted Places in Kendallville, Indiana." Haunted Places, Indiana State University. https://www.hauntedplaces.org/.

"Indiana Hauntings." This Is Indiana. October 16, 2013. https://thisisindiana.angelfire.com/indianahauntings.htm.

James, J., and J. Stanley. *Common Mystics Podcast*. https://commonmystics.net/.

McEwen, W.H. *History of Northeast Indiana*. The Lewis Publishing Company, 1920.

Meek, B. "Searching for the Erie-Michigan Canal." *Indiana Waterways* 11, no. 1 (October 1, 1982): n.p.

Mott, M.H. *History of the Regulators of Northern Indiana*. Indianapolis Journal Company, 1859.

"Noble County Cemetery Records." LDS Genealogy. https://ldsgenealogy.com/IN/Noble-County-Cemetery-Records.htm.

"Noble County Indiana History and Genealogy." Genealogy Trails. http://genealogytrails.com/ind/noble/index.html.

"Plat Book and Statistical Record of Noble County, Indiana." LDS Genealogy, Library of Congress. https://www.loc.gov/resource/g4093nm.gla00026/?st=gallery.

"Rome City, Indiana Ghost Encounter." OMG, Did You Hear That? https://omgdidyouhearthat.com/2020/10/15/rome-city-indiana-ghost-encounter/.

Roof, G.W. *Popular History of Noble County Capitals and Greater Albion*. New Era Publishing House, 1908.

"Sand Hill (Noble County, Indiana)." *Wikipedia*. April 19, 2017. https://en.wikipedia.org/wiki/Sand_Hill_(Noble_County,_Indiana)

Smith, J.M. "Blacklegs, Regulators and the Hanging of Gregory McDougle." *Indiana History Bulletin* 46, no. 9 (September 1969): 3. https://indianamemory.contentdm.oclc.org/digital/collection/p16066coll16/id/14143/.

"Spook Light Hill." ISU Special Collections, Indiana State University. March 30, 2011. https://indstate.contentdm.oclc.org/digital/collection/folklore/id/1141

About the Authors

Mark and Emily Hunter live in Albion, Indiana, the dead center of Noble County, where he works as a 911 dispatcher and she wrangles horses at the Pokagon State Park Saddle Barn. They are the authors of twelve books, both fiction and nonfiction.